A SIMPLE START TO JQUERY, JAVASCRIPT, AND HTML5 FOR BEGINNERS

SCOTT SANDERSON

CONTENTS

1

INTRODUCTION

If there is one application development framework that can be termed as comprehensive, then HTML5 wins the bid hands down. Although, the specification for HTML5 is not yet complete, most modern web browsers support the popular features on device, which range from a Smartphone to a desktop. What that means is that you just have to write one application and it will run on your devices without any interoperability issues.

There is no doubt about the fact that HTML5 is the future of web application development and if you wish to remain in the league, you need to think futuristically and equip yourself to deal the technological challenges that the future is about to throw at you. The scope of HTML5 is evident from the fact that most of the major players of the industry and setting their eyes on this technology and giving in full support to the same.

If the multi-faceted functionality and high-on features characteristics of HTML5 intrigue you and you want to start writing your own applications right away, but you do not know how and where to begin, then this book is just for you. This book covers everything that you shall require to create working applications with the help of HTML, JavaScript/JQuery and CSS. However, it is not a reference guide. We hope to give you practical knowledge so that you can get to development as quickly as possible.

This book is a perfect start-up guide and covers all the basic facets of HTML5, JavaScript and CSS development. It covers everything from the very basics to all that you shall require in your tryst with this framework. The first three chapters introduce you to these three technologies, giving you some ground to start with.

BASICS OF HTML5

HTML (Hyper Text Markup Language) is a language used for creating web pages. In fact, this language has been in use since the first webpage was made. However, the functionality has evolved as newer and better versions of the language were introduced. The language is known to have originated from SGML (Standard Generalized Markup Language), which was earlier used for document publishing. HTML has inherited the concept of formatting features and their syntax from SGML.

One of the most interesting and beneficial facet of HTML usage, as far as browsers are concerned, is that browsers support both backward as well as forward compatibility. While backward compatibility is usually easy to achieve, forward compatibility is tricky as the problem domain, in this case, is infinitely large. However, in order to implement this, browsers were designed to ignore tags that it did not recognize.

For years, HTML remained all that people wanted. However, with time, people felt the need for more, which was catalyzed by the presence of another technology called

XML (eXtensible Markup Language). Although, XML shares a lot of similarities with HTML, there exist many fundamental differences between the two. Firstly, XML requires tag matching in the sense that for every starting tag, a closing tag must inevitably exist. Besides this, XML allow you to create your own tags as it does not possess a fixed set of tags like HTML.

The tags used in XML are meta-tags or tags that describe the data that is included between the starting and closing tag. In order to ensure the validity of the XML document, a technology called XSD (XML Schema Definition) is used. However, this technology cannot be used for validating HTML documents because HTML documents lack a well-defined structure.

The W3C (World Wide Web Consortium) introduced XHTML as an attempt to fix the flaws of HTML. According to the XHTML specification, HTML documents were forced to adhere to the format specifications used for XML. Therefore, this allowed the use of XSD tools for validation of HTML documents. Although, the integration of XML in the framework fixed some issues, some issues continued to crop up. One of the staggering issues of the modern times was the growing need for integration of multimedia. While CSS did perform formatting of some level, it was becoming inadequate for the growing demands of users.

IN ORDER TO provide support for interactivity and animated visuals, a programmable support called JavaScript was added to this ensemble. However, initial versions of this support were difficult for programmers to understand and slow on execution time incurred. This led to the introduction of plug-ins like Flash to get the attention that it did. These plugins did what was expected of them, but the browser-multimedia integration was still loose in nature.

HTML5 is not an evolved form of XHTML. On the contrary, HTML5 can be better described as the reinvented form of HTML 4.01 and how HTML, CSS and JavaScript can be used together to solve the growing needs of the user base.

Semantic Markup

The fundamental feature of HTML5 is that it stresses on separation of behaviour, presentation and structure. The semantic markup of a website development specifies the structure of the document. In other words, it specifies the meaning of tags and what they will do for you. On the other hand, behaviour and presentation are governed by CSS and JavaScript respectively.

HTML5 Elements

In HTML, an element is simply a statement that contains a beginning tag, content and a closing tag. Therefore, when you write,

```
<div>
<b>This is my world!</b>
</div>
```

In this example, the div elements includes everything from <div> to </div>. therefore, the <b></b> tag is also a part of the div element.

It is important to state here that HTML5 is not case sensitive. Therefore, regardless of whether you write <B> or <b> for the bold tag, the browser will consider the two same. However, the use of lower case for tags is recommended by the W3C standards.

Working with Elements in HTML5

HTML5 defines more than a 100 elements. These elements, with their definitions are provided in Appendix.

How to add attributes to elements?

Additional data can be added to the begin tag in the form of attributes. An attribute can be generally represented as, name="value". The value for the attribute name is enclosed within quotes. There is no restriction on the number of attributes that can be added to the begin tag. For these attributes, the attribute has a name, but it does not have a value.

Example:

<div id="main" class="mainContent"></div>

Here, id and class are attributes where id uniquely identifies the element and class specifies the CSS style to which this div belongs.

Boolean Attributes

Several types of attributes can be used. One of the most commonly used types is Boolean attribute. The Boolean attribute can take a value from the allowable set of values. Some possible values include:

- Checked
- Disabled
- Selected
- Readonly

There are two ways to indicate the value of a Boolean attribute.

<input type="checkbox" name="vegetable" value="Broccoli" checked="" />

<input type="checkbox" name="vegetable" value="Broccoli" checked='checked' />

In the first case, the value is not given and is assumed.

Although, the latter seems like a redundant form, it is the more preferred form, particularly if you are using jQuery.

Global Attribute Reference

There is a set of named attributes available in HTML5, which can be used with any element. Examples of these attributes include accesskey, spellcheck and draggable, in addition to several others.

Void Elements

Some elements do not have to contain content under any circumstance. These elements include <link>, <br> and <area>, in addition to many others.

Self-closing Tags

If you are using an element that does not contain any content, then you can use a self closing tag. An example of this tag is <br/>. However, please note that other tags like <div> have to be written as <div></div> even if they do not have any content.

How to Add Expando Attributes

Any attribute that you as the author define is known as expando attribute. You can give this custom attribute a name and assign a value to the same as and when required.

How to Add Comments

Comments can be added using a ! and two hyphens (-). The syntax for adding comments is as follows:

<!—text -->

You can also add conditional comments using the following syntax:

<!--[if lte IE 7]> <html class="no-js ie6" lang="en"> <![endif]-->

This comment determines if the browser being used is an earlier version released earlier than IE7.

How to Create HTML Document

An HTML document can simply be described as a frame that contains metadata, content and a structure.

The HTML document must start with the tag <!DOC-TYPE html>. In HTML5, the declaration is an indication to the browser that it should work in no-quirks mode or HTML5 compliant mode.

The next tag should be <html>. This element includes within itself the elements <head> and <body>. The <head> element can contain the metadata for the HTML document, which is declared and defined using the <meta> tag. The <head> element also contains the <title> element, which serves the following purposes:

- Used by search engines
- This content is displayed in the browser toolbar
- Gives a default name to the page.

The <body> element includes any other information that is to be displayed on the HTML document.

A sample HTML document is given below:

```
<!DOCTYPE html>
<html>
<head>
<meta charset="utf-8" />
<title>TITLE OF DOC</title>
</head>
<body>
CONTENT
</body>
</html>
```

Note:

1. Special character like '>' or '<', which are a part

of the HTML syntax, can be used on the HTML doc using their name or number. The syntax for their usage is:

&entity_name or &entity_number

The appendix contains the table of entity names and numbers to be used.

1. White space created using tabs, line breaks and spaces is normalized by HTML into a single space. Therefore, if you want to use multiple spaces, you must use the non-breaking space character. For example, if you want to display 10 mph such that 10 and mph are not separated by a newline, you can write 10 mph.

How to Embed Content

Now that you know how to create HTML documents with your content, you may want to embed content into the document from other sources. This content may be text from another HTML document or flash applications.

Inline Frames

Inline frames are used to embed HTML documents inline with the content of the current HTML document. Therefore, in a way, this element creates nested browsers as multiple web page are loaded in the same window. These are implemented using the <iframe> element. Nested browsing contexts can be navigated using:

- window.parent – This WindowProxy object represents the parent browsing context.
- window.top – This WindowProxy object represents the top-level browsing context

- window.frameElement – This represents the browsing context container and if there is no context container, it returns null.

The syntax of the <iframe> element is as follows:

<iframe src="name"></iframe>

Here the name of the attribute defines the name of the browsing context. This name can be any string like 'sample.html'. However, the strong should not start with an underscore as names starting with underscore are reserved for special key names like _blank.

Sandboxing

Sandboxing is used for avoiding the introduction of pop-ups or any other malware in your HTML document. In order to implement this, the attribute 'sandbox' is used. You can use this attribute in the following manner:

<iframe sandbox="keywords" src="name">

</iframe>

When you use sandboxing, several restrictions are imposed on the called context. These restrictions include disabling forms, scripts, plugins and any frame other than itself. You can force the system to override these restrictions using keywords like:

- allow-same-origin
- allow-scripts
- allow-forms
- allow-top-navigation

Multiple keywords can be used by separating them using a space.

Seamless Embedding

The seamless attribute can be used in the <iframe>

element for embedding of content in a manner than this content appears to be part of the main content. This attribute can be used in the following manner:

<iframe seamless="" src="name"></iframe>

<iframe seamless src="name"></iframe>

<iframe seamless="seamless" src="name"></iframe>

This attribute may not be supported by many browsers. Therefore, you can use CSS to achieve a similar effect.

Hyperlinks

Hyperlinks can be implemented using the <a> element. This element can be used to link both external (a different HTML document) as well as internal (another location in the same HTML document) links.

All links are underlined and depending upon the nature of the link, the colour of the link changes.

- Blue - Unvisited link
- Purple - Visited link
- Red - Active link

The first attribute of the <a> element is href, which is given the value of the URL.

Syntax for external links:

<a href="address">Text</a>

Syntax for internal links:

<a href="#id">Text</a>

The id here is the id of the tag to which you want the link to jump onto. However, if you use only the # value, the link jumps to the top of the page.

The other attribute used with the <a> element is target, which allows you to control the behaviour of the link. For instance, if you want the link to open in another window, then this requirement can be specified using this attribute. The following can be used:

- _blank

This opens the link in a new browser window.

- _parent

This opens the link in the parent window.

- _self

This opens the link in the current window and is the default setting.

- _top

This opens the link in the topmost frame of the current window.

- <iframe_name>

This opens the link in the *<iframe>* element of the specified name. This is generally used in menus.

Hyperlinks can also be used to send emails using the following syntax:

<a href="mailto:email address">Text</a>

When the user clicks on the link, an email will be sent to the specified email address.

Embedding Images

The <img> element is used for adding images to the

HTML document. The <img> tag is a void element and does not require a closing tag.

The required tag for this element is *src*, which specifies the absolute or relative address at which the image is stored. Another attribute than can be used with the <img> tag is *target*, which is used to specify the text that must be displayed in case the image is not available.

Syntax:

<img src="address" target="alternative text">

It is important to note that you only give references to images and they are not embedded into the HTML document, in actuality. The allowed image formats are jpeg, svg, png and gif.

How to Create Image Map

The <map> element can be used to create a clickable image map. In order to create a link between the map and image, you must set a name of the map and use this name in the usemap attribute of the img tag.

The area of the map element is defined using <area> element. This is a self-closing tag that is used to define the area of the map. The area of the map can be set using the attributes shape, href, alt and coords.

The shape attribute can be give the values poly, circle, rect or default. The default value sets the area as the size of the image. The href and alt attributes are used in the same manner as they are used in the <a> element. Lastly, the coords attribute are defined according to the shape chosen in the following manner:

- poly – $x_1, y_1, x_2, y_2, ..., x_n, y_n$
- circle – x, y, radius
- rect - x_1, y_1, x_2, y_2

For the polygon, the starting and ending coordinates should be the same. In case a discrepancy in this regard exists, a closing value is added.

Example:

<img src ="worldmap.gif" width="145" height="126" alt="World Map" usemap ="#country" />

<map name="country">

<area shape="circle" coords="105,50,30" href="China.html" alt="China" />

<area   shape="default"   href="InvalidCountry.html" alt="Please Try Again" />

</map>

Embedding Plug-ins

Plugins can likewise be embedded into HTML documents using <embed> and <object> elements. Although, both these elements perform similar tasks, they were created by different browsers. As a result, they coexist in HTML5. While the <embed> element provides ease of use, the <object> element provides more functionality to the user. Syntax for these two elements is given below:

The <embed> tag

<embed src="Flash.swf"> </embed>

The src attribute specifies the url or address of the file to be embedded. Other attributes that are taken by the <embed> element includes:

- type - used to specify the MIME type of the content
- height – used to specify the content height in pixels
- width – used to specify the content width in pixels

As mentioned previously, some browsers may not support <embed> element. Therefore, if you are using it in your document, you must add fallback content specification. For instance, if you are embedding a flash file, you must redirect the user to the download link of flash player if the browser does not support it already.

You can do this in the following manner:

<embed src="Flash.swf" >

<a href="link for downloading flash player">

<img src="address of the image for download flash player"

alt="Download Adobe Flash player" />

</a>

</embed>

The <object> tag

The <object> tag allows you to embed a variety of multimedia files like video, audio, PDF, applets and Flash. The element accepts the following attributes:

- type – used to specify the MIME type of data
- form – used to specify the form id or ids of the object
- data – used to specify the URL of the resources that the object uses
- usemap – used to specify the name of a client-side image map that the object uses
- name – used to specify the object name
- height – used to specify the height of the object in pixels
- width – used to specify the width of the object in pixels

Of all the attributes mentioned above, it is necessary to mention either the data or type attribute.

Data can be passed into the <object> element using the <param> tag, which is a combination of name and value attributes. Multiple parameters can be declared using this tag.

```
<object data="file.wav">
<param name="autoplay" value="false" />
</object>
```

Note:

1. The <object> element must always be used inside the <body> element.
2. HTML5 supports only the attributes listed above and global attributes for the <object> element.

3

BASICS OF JAVASCRIPT

Interaction is an important facet of any website. In order to connect with the audience in a better way, it is vital to add behaviour to the website. This can be as simple as buttons or as complex as animations. These tasks can be added using JavaScript, which is a web and programming language. This chapter introduces JavaScript and shall help you get started with JavaScript on an immediate basis.

Background

JavaScript is the preferred programming language for client side scripting. Contrary to popular belief, JavaScript is in no way related to Java. In fact, it finds resemblance to ECMAScript. Besides this, the only common thing between this programming language and other programming languages like C and C++ is that it uses curly braces. The international standard for JavaScript is given in ISO/IEC 16262 and ECMA-262 specification.

One of the most important features of this programming language is that it is untyped. In other words, specifying the type of a variable is not necessary for using it. For example, if you have assigned a string to a variable, you can later assign an integer to the same variable. Variables are declared using the keyword *var*.

Data and Expressions

Any program accesses, manipulates and represents data to the user. Data is available in different types and forms. This data can be easily decomposed into values. In JavaScript, data may be represented as a primitive value, object or function.

The data representation at the lowest level is known as primitive data type and includes null, undefined, number, string and Boolean.

Several built-in objects are defined in JavaScript. These entail the Object object, global object, Array object, Function object, Boolean object, String object, Math object, Number object, the RegExp object, Date object, Error object and JSON object.

Any object that is callable is called a function. It may also be referred to as a method if the function is associated with an object.

Data is produced by using expressions, which is a name given to any code that generates a value. It may be assigned a value directly or the value may be computed by substituting and computing an expression composed of operands and operators. It is important to note that an operand can be another expression as well.

Number Data Type

The number data type is a primitive data type and it is internally stored as a floating point number, which is a 64 bit, double precision number. This 64 bit field stores the sign, exponent and fraction. While the leftmost bit is reserved for sign, the bits 0 to 51 are reserved for storing the fraction and bits 52-62 are used for the exponent.

Because of memory limitation on the system, 2^{53} is the

highest integer that can be stored. It is important to note that integer calculations generate a precise value. However, fractional data calculation may give imprecise results. Therefore, these values have to be truncated.

In addition to numbers and strings, JavaScript also supports the use of the following special characters.

- undefined specifies that the value has not been assigned yet.
- *NaN stands for* 'Not a Number'
- -Infinity any number that is less than -1.7976931348623157E + 10308 is denoted by Infinity.
- Infinity - any number that exceeds the value 1.7976931348623157E + 10308 is denoted by Infinity.

String Data Type

A string can simply be described as a collection of characters. Whenever you declare character(s) within quotes, the system interprets as a string. Sample strings include:

'Hello World!'

"Hello World!"

However, if you want to include quotes as characters in the string, then you must add '\' before the character. Sample string:

'You\'re Welcome'

"You\'re Welcome"

JavaScript also supports other escape sequences like \t for tab and \n for newline.

Boolean Data Type

The Boolean data type is a binary data type and return

either true or false. These operators are commonly used to indicate results of comparisons. For example,

10 > 5 will give 'true' while 5 > 10 will give 'false'.

Operations on Number data Type

In order to perform calculations, operators are used. JavaScript supports all the basic operators and the operator precedence is as follows:

- Addition and subtraction have the same precedence.
- Multiplication and division have the same precedence.
- The precedence of multiplication and division is higher than that of addition and subtraction.
- If an expression contains several operators of the same precedence, then the expression is evaluated from left to right.

In addition to the basic operators, JavaScript also supports modulo (%) operator. This operator performs division and returns the remainder as result. For example, 23%7 is equal to 2.

Unary Operators

While operators like addition and subtraction need to operands to execute, some operators require only one. An example of such operators is *typeof*, which returns the datatype of the data. For example, *typeof* 12 returns 'number'. Please note that '+' and '-' can also be used as unary operators. This is the case when they are used to specify the sign of a number.

Logical Operators

Three logical operators are available for use in Java-Script namely, Not (!), Or (||) and And (&&). The results of operations that involve these operators are Boolean (true or false). The results of these operations are computed in accordance with the following:

AND (&&)

Binary operator

Both the conditions must be true

OR (||)

Binary operator

At least one of the conditions must be true

NOT (!)

Unary operator

The value of the condition determined is complemented.

For example,

'Red' != 'Blue' && 5 > 1 = 'true'

'Red' != 'Blue' && 5 < 1 = 'false'

'Red' == 'Blue' && 5 < 1 = 'false'

For conditional operators, JavaScript uses short-circuit evaluation. In other words, if the value of the first condition is computed to be 'false', the system does not evaluate the other condition and directly presents the result.

Writing Code in JavaScript

Any statement followed by a semicolon is referred to as a statement. This statement may or may not produce a value unlike expressions, which must inadvertently produce a value.

Variables

Manipulation of data is performed with the help of variables. Data is stored in the memory and a named reference to this memory location is called a variable. Any identifier is declared as a variable by preceding it with a keyword *var*. A sample declaration of a variable is:

var result;

This statement declares a variable *result*. You may also define the variable as you declare it using a statement like this:

var result = 0;

or

*var result = 23*4+6;*

Certain rules have to be followed while naming variables. These rules are as follows:

- A variable name can be a combination of numbers and characters.
- A variable name cannot start with a number.
- The only special characters allowed in variable names is underscore (_) and dollar sign($).
- There should not be any whitespace in the variable name. For example, 'result value' is not allowed.
- JavaScript keywords are reserved and cannot be used.

Please note that JavaScript, unlike HTML is case sensitive. Therefore VAL and val are two different variables. Also, it is recommended that the variable name should be such that it describes the purpose for which it is being used. For example, if we name a variable result, it is evident that this variable will contain the result value computed by the code.

Another convention used in JavaScript is to name variables such that the first letter of the variable name is lowercase. However, every subsequent word in variable name starts with a capital letter. An example of this is the variable name, arrayResult. Besides this, the use of underscore and dollar sign is discouraged. However, they are used in jQuery objects.

Environment

A complete set of variables and the values they contain form what is called the environment. Therefore, whenever you load a new webpage in the browser, you are creating a new environment. If you take the example of Windows 8, it creates an environment when an application starts and the same is destroyed when the application ends.

Functions

A set of statements that solve a purpose are referred to as a function. The purpose of using functions is code reuse. If your program uses functionality multiple times in the program, then it is implemented as a function, which can be called as and when required. Since, a function is to be called from within the code, parameters can be sent to the function from the code. Upon execution, the function returns a value to the calling function. The syntax for function declaration and definition is as follows:

```
function multiply(a, b){
return a*b;
}
```

The name of the function must always be preceded with the keyword function. The variables a and b are parameters passed into the function and the function return the value obtained by computing a*b. This is a simple function, but you can implement complex and large function depending upon the functionality desired.

Now that you have implemented the function, you must be wondering as to how the function is called. Here is an example:

```
var x=2;
var y=5
```

var c=multiply(x, y);

Here, x and y are arguments that the function multiply will receive as parameters.

JavaScript is a loosely typed language. What that means is that if you pass more arguments to a function than what it is expecting, the system simply uses the first n arguments required and discards the rest. The advantage of this functionality is that you can use already implemented functions and pass the extra argument to scale the function and add functionality to it. On the other hand, you will not be able to get any indication of error if you unintentionally pass the wrong number of arguments.

JavaScript also provides some built-in functions for interacting with the user. These functions are as follows:

• alert

This function raises an alert with a message and the system resumes operation after the user clicks on the OK button. Sample implementation:

alert('Alert message!');

• prompt

This function presents a textbox to the user and asks him or her to give input. You can supply the default value in the presented textbox and the user can click on the OK button to accept that the value entered is correct. Sample implementation:

var result = prompt('Enter a value', 'default value');

• confirm

This message gives the user the choice to OK or CANCEL an action. Sample implementation:

var result = confirm('Do you wish to proceed?');

Function Scope

Each variable that you declare possesses a scope of operation, which is the function within which the variable has been declared. This is called the local scope. Unlike, many other languages, which define local scope by the curly braces within which the variable lies, JavaScript's local scope is same as function scope.

In addition to this, JavaScript also supports the concept of global scope, in which variables can be declared global and thus, can be used anywhere in the program.

Nesting Functions

Functions can be nested at any level. In other words, a function can be called from within another function, which could have been called from a different function. However, it is important to note that the scope of variable is within the function in which they are declared.

Conversion of One Data Type to Another

The prompt function discussed in the previous function returns a string. However, you had asked the user to enter a number. In such a scenario, a string to number conversion may be required. In JavaScript, a variable can be converted from one type to another using the following functions:

- Number Function

This function converts the object supplied to it into number data type. However, if the function is unable to perform the conversion, *NaN* is returned.

- String Function

This function converts the object supplied to it into string data type.

Conditional Programming

While writing code, you will faced with several situation where you need to execute a different set of instructions if the condition is true and another set of instructions if the same is false.

if-else

In order to implement such scenarios, you can use the if-else construct.

Syntax:

```
If(condition)
{
//code
}
else
{
//code
}
```

Consider a scenario in which you ask the user to enter his or her age using prompt function. Now, you must validate if the age is a valid number, before performing any computation on the value supplied. This is an ideal scenario of implementing conditional programming. Sample implementation for this scenario is:

```
var userAge = prompt('Enter your age: ', '');
if(isNaN(userAge))
{
alert('Age entered is invalid!');
}
else
{
//code
```

```
}
```

In this sample code, the if clause checks if the entered value is a number. If the condition is true, that is the object entered is not a number, the user is given an alert message. However, if the condition is false, the code for else is executed.

It is important to note here that for single statements, it is not necessary to use curly braces. The above mentioned code can also be written as:

```
var userAge = prompt('Enter your age: ', '');
if(isNaN(userAge))
alert('Age entered is invalid!');
else
//code
```

However, it is a good practice to use curly braces as there is scope of adding additional code later on.

if-else if

Another conditional programming construct is if-else if construct. This construct allows you to declare multiple conditions and the actions associated with them. The syntax is:

```
if(condition)
{
//code
}
else if(condition)
{
//code
}
else
{
//code
}
```

Switch

Multiple else ifs can be implemented using this construct. The execution overhead is high for this conditional programming construct as conditions are sequentially checked for validity. As an alternative, another keyword, switch, is available, which implements multiple conditions in the form of a jump table. Therefore, the execution overhead for switch is lesser than that of if-else if.

Sample implementation:

```
var userChoice = prompt('Choose an alphabet: a, b, c', 'e');
switch (userChoice) {
case 'a':
alert('a chosen\n');
break;
case 'b':
alert('b chosen\n');
break;
case 'c':
alert('c chosen\n');
break;
default:
alert('None of the alphabets chosen\n');
break;
};
```

The switch construct matches that value entered by the user with the values presented in the cases. If a matching value is found, the case is executed. However, in case, none of the case values match the entered input, the default case is executed. Besides this, you can also use conditions in case values and the case for which the condition holds true is executed.

If you do not use the break statement after the code of a

case, all the cases following the matching case will be executed. For example, if the user enters 'b' for the above example and there are no break statements after the case code, then the output will be:

b chosen

c chosen

None of the alphabets chosen

Also, it is a good practice to use a break statement in the default case as well.

Note:

If you wish to determine if a keyword has been assigned any value or not, you can use the following code:

```
if(c)
{
//code
}
else
{
//code
}
```

If the variable c has been assigned a not-null value, then the if condition is true and the corresponding code is executed. On the other hand, if the value of variable c is undefined or null, the code within the else construct is executed.

Note:

The value of the following conditions will always be true:

```
" == 0
null == undefined
'123' == 123
false == 0;
```

Please note that JavaScript converts the type of the variable concerned for compatibility in comparisons.

However, if you want to compare both the value and type of two variables, then JavaScript provides another set of operators, === and !===. When the comparisons for the values mentioned in the above example are done using this operator, the resultant will always be false.

Implementing Code Loops

Looping is an important and commonly used construct of any programming language. You will be faced by several situations when you need to perform the same set of instructions, a given number of times. In order to implement this scenario, loops have to be used. Loop constructs available in JavaScript include for, while and do-while.

The while loop includes a condition and as long as the condition remains true, the loop continues to execute. The do – while loop is a modification of the while loop. If the condition in the while is false, the while loop will not execute at all. On the other hand, even if the while condition is false, the do-while loop executes at least once.

Syntax for while loop:

```
while(condition)
{
//code
}
```

Syntax for do-while loop:

```
do
{
//code
}
while(condition)
```

The last type of loop available in JavaScript is for loop. The for loop allows you to initialize the looping variable, check for condition and modify the looping variable in the same statement.

Syntax:

```
for(initialize; condition; modify)
{
//code
}
```

Sample code:

```
for(i=0; i<10; i=i+1)
{
//code
}
```

This loop will run 10 times.

Note:

1. If at any point in time, you wish the loop to break, you can use the break statement.
2. If you do not specify a condition or specify a condition that is always true, the loop will run infinitely.

Error Handling

Exceptions are expected to occur at several points in your code. Therefore, it is best to implement a mechanism that can help you deal with these exceptions and avoid crashing.

An exception can be described as an illegal operation or any condition that is unexpected and not ordinary. A few examples of exceptions include unauthorized memory access.

You can perform exception handling at your own level by validating the values of variables before performing any operations. for instance, before performing division, it is advisable to check if the value of the denominator is equal to zero. Any operation that involves division of a number by zero raises the divide-by-zero exception.

However, there are other situations that cannot be handled in this manner. For instance, if the network connection breaks abruptly, you cannot do anything to pre-emptively handle the situation. Therefore, for situations like these, try, catch and finally keywords are used.

The code that is expected to throw an exception is put inside the try block. This exception, upon its occurrence, is caught by the catch block, which executes code that is supposed to be executed immediately after an exception is caught. The catch may also be followed by the finally block, which performs the final cleanup. This block is executed after the execution of try and catch blocks.

Syntax:

```
try
{
//code
}
catch(exception name)
{
//code
}
finally
{
//code
}
```

Working with Objects

JavaScript allows user access to a number of existing objects. One of these objects is an array. This section discusses all the basics related to this chapter. Dealing with objects in JavaScript also includes creation and handling of customized objects. However, this topic shall be covered in the chapter on JavaScript and jQuery.

Arrays

A collection of similar objects that are sequenced contiguously are referred to as an array. This array is given a name and each element can be accessed using the indexer, in the following form:

Let arrName[] be an array of names. The element arrName[2] refers to the third element of the array.

An array can be created using the following three methods:

- Insertion of Items Using Indexer

An array can be created using the new keyword and then, elements can be added into the array by assigning values to independent elements of the array. The new keyword creates an instance of the object Array using the constructor for the same.

Sample implementation:

var arrName = new Array();
arrName [0] = 'Jack';
arrName [1] = 'Alex';

- Condensed Array

The second type of implementation also uses the new keyword. However, in this case, the values are assigned to the elements as arguments to the constructor of the Array object.

Sample implementation:

var arrName = new Array('Jack, 'Alex');

- Literal Array

In this type of array definition, values are provided within the square brackets.

Sample implementation:

var arrName = ['Jack, 'Alex'];

The advantage of using the first type of definition is that it allows you to assign values to the elements anywhere in the code. On the other hand, the second and third type of implementation requires you to have the exact list of elements with you beforehand.

There are some properties associated with all object. The one property that can come in handy to you is *length,* which is a read-only value and when called return the number of elements present in the array. You can use this property in loops and conditions.

Objects can also have their own functions. These functions are called methods. The methods available for Array include:

- concat

Returns an array, which is the concatenation of the two arrays supplied to it.

- indexOf

Finds the location of the element concerned in the array and returns the index of the same.

- join

This method concatenates all the values present in the

array. However, all these values are separated by a comma by default. You can specify a delimiter of your choice as well.

- lastIndexOf

This method works similarly as indexOf. However, it performs the search from the last element of the array. Therefore, it returns the index of the last element that matches the specified criterion.

- pop

Removes the last element and returns its value.

- push

Adds the concerned element to the end of the array and returns the changed value of length.

- reverse

This method reverses the order of the array elements. The original array is modified by this method.

- shift

Removes and returns the first value. If the array is empty, then undefined is returned.

- slice

This method requires two arguments, start index and

end index. A new array is created with elements same as the elements present at indexes (start index) and (end index – 1).

- sort

This method sorts the elements and modifies the original array.

- splice

This method removes and adds elements to the specified array. The arguments taken by this method are start index (index from where the system should start removing elements), number of elements to be removed and elements to be added. If the value passed for number of elements is 0, then no elements are deleted. On the other hand, if this value is greater than the size of the array, all elements from the start index to the end of the array are deleted.

- toString

This method creates a string, which is a comma separated concatenated string of all the elements present in the array.

- unshift

This method adds an element at the first location of the array and return the modified value of length.

- valueOf

This method returns a string, which is the concatenated, comma-separated string containing all the values present in the array.

Note:

1. When working with functions, you can pass the whole array (using the array name) or a particular element of the array (using array name[indexer]).

2. Array elements can be modified by accessing the element using the indexer. For example, arrName[1] = 'Danny'; assigns the value 'Danny' to the second element of the array.

DOM objects

The primary objects that you need to access while building an application, are the DOM objects associated with it. This access is necessary for you to control and get notified about events that are occurring on the webpage.

The DOM is a representation of a hierarchy of objects. These objects can be accessed using the *document* variable, which is built-in. This variable references the DOM and performs a search, which may return an active or static *NodeList*. While the active NodeList contains a list of elements that keep changing, the static NodeList contains elements that do not change over time. Since the retrieval of the static NodeList takes longer, it is advisable to choose search methods that work with active NodeList.

The search methods available for DOM include:

- getElementById

This method returns a reference to the first element that has the specified ID.

- getElementsByTagName

This method returns the active NodeList, which has the specified tag name.

- getElementsByName

This method returns the active NodeList, which has the specified name. This is a preferred method for option buttons.

- getElementsByClass

This method returns the active NodeList, which has the specified class name. However, this method is not supported by Internet Explorer version 8 and earlier.

- querySelector

This method accepts CSS selector as parameter and return the first matched element. However, this method is not supported by Internet Explorer version 7 and earlier.

- querySelectorAll

This method accepts CSS selector as parameter and return all the matched elements. Therefore, it returns a static NodeList. However, this method is not supported by Internet Explorer version 7 and earlier.

Events

If you look at JavaScript as an engine, then events are what give it the required spark. Events can occur in two situations. The first type of events are those that occur during user interactions. A user may click an image or enter text. All these are classified as events. Besides this, changes in state of the system are also considered an event. For instance, if a video starts or stops, an event is said to have occurred. The DOM allows you to capture events and execute code for the same.

In JavaScript, events are based on the publish-subscribe methodology. Upon creation of an object, the developer can publish the events that are related to this object. Moreover, event handlers can be added to this object whenever it is used. The event handler function notifies the subscribed events that the event has been triggered. This notification includes information about the event like location of the mouse and key-presses, in addition to several other details relevant to the event.

Capturing events:

There may be situations when an event may be attached to a button click, which may lie inside a hyperlink. In this situation, there is nesting of elements. Therefore, the event, when triggered, is passed down the DOM hierarchy. This process is called event capturing. However, once the event has reached the element, this event is bubbled up the hierarchy. This process is called event bubbling. This movement of the event across the hierarchy gives the developer an opportunity to subscribe or cancel the propagation, on need basis.

Subscribing to event:

The function, addEventListener, can be used for the subscription process. This function requires three arguments, the event, the function that needs to be called for the event and a Boolean value that determines if the function will be called during the capture or bubble process (true – capture, false – bubble). Mostly, this value is set to false. This is the preferred method for subscription as it is mentioned in the W3C standard.

Sample Code:

var btn = document.getElementById('btnDownload');

btn.addEventListener('click', initiateDownload, false);

However, other methods also exist, which include giving an online subscription to the html tag. This subscribes the event to the bubble process. The advantage of using this method is that it is the oldest and most accepted method. therefore, you can be sure that this method will work, regardless of what browser you are using. Please see the tag below to understand how this can be done.

<button   id='btnDownload'   onclick='initiateDownload();' >Download</button>

You can also use the traditional subscription process that uses JavaScript for subscribing the event.

var btn = document.getElementById('btnDownload');

btn.onclick = initiateDownload;

Unsubscribing:

Events can be unsubscribed using the function, removeEventListener, which takes the same set of parameters as addEventListener. For the btn variable used in the previous example, this can be done in the following manner:

var btn = document.getElementById('btnDownload');

btn.removeEventListener('click',   initiateDownload, false);

How to cancel propagation?

The function, stopPropagation, is used for performing this operation. This can be done in the following manner:

```
var btn = document.getElementById('btnDownload');
btn.addEventListener('click', initiateDownload, false);
function initiateDownload (e){
//download
e.stopPropagation();
}
```

How to prevent the default operation?

This can be done by using the function, preventDefault, in the following manner:

```
var hyperlink = document.getElementById('linkSave');
hyperlink.addEventListener('click', saveData, false);
function saveData(e){
//save data
e.preventDefault();
}
```

JavaScript also provides the *this* keyword, which can be used if you wish to access the event causing element, on a frequent basis.

Window Event Reference

The current browser window is represented by the window variable, which is an instance of the Window object. The following events are associated with this object:

- afterprint
- beforeonload
- beforeprint
- error
- blur
- haschange
- load
- message
- focus
- online

- offline
- pageshow
- pagehide
- redo
- popstate
- storage
- resize
- unload
- undo

Form Event Reference

The actions that occur inside an HTML form trigger the flowing events:

- change
- blur
- focus
- contextmenu
- forminput
- formchange
- invalid
- input
- submit
- select

Keyboard Event Reference

The keyboard triggers the following events:

- keyup
- keypress
- keydown

Mouse Event Reference

The mouse triggers the following events:

- click
- drag
- drop
- scroll
- dblclick
- dragenter
- dragstart
- dragend
- dragover
- dragleave
- mousemove
- mousedown
- mouseover
- mouseout
- mousewheel
- mouseup

Media Event Reference

Media elements like videos, images and audios also trigger events, which are as follows:

- canplay
- abort
- waiting
- durationchange
- canplaythrough
- ended
- emptied
- loadeddata
- error
- loadstart

- loadedmetadata
- play
- pause
- progress
- playing
- readystatechange
- ratechange
- seeking
- seeked
- suspend
- stalled
- volumechange
- timeupdate

4

BASICS OF CSS3

Cascading Style Sheets or CSS provide the presentation that webpages are known for. Although, HTML is capable of providing a basic structure to the webpage, CSS offers developers host of design options. Besides this, it is fast and efficient, which makes it an all more popular design tool.

CSS is known to have evolved from SGML (Standardized Generalized Markup

Language). The goal of efforts made in this direction was to standardize the manner in which web pages looked. The latest version of this technology is CSS3, which is a collection of 50 modules.

The most powerful characteristic of CSS is its cascading ability. Simply, it allows a webpage to take its styles from multiple sheets in such a manner that changes to the style in subsequently read sheets overwrite the style already implemented from one or more of the previous sheets.

How to Define and Apply Style

The definition and application of a style involves two facets or parts, selector and declaration. While the selector determines the area of the webpage that needs to be styled, the declaration block describes the style specifications that have to be implemented. In order to illustrate how it works, let us consider the following example,

body {
color: white;
}

In this example, the selector selects the body of the webpage and the declaration block defines that the font color should be changed to white. This is a simple example and declarations and selectors can be much more complex than this.

How to Add Comments

Comments can be added to the style sheet using the following format:

/*write the comment here*/

How to Create an Inline Style

Every element has an associated global attribute, style. This global attribute can be manipulated within the tag for that element to modify the appearance of that element. This type of styling does not require you to specify the selector. Only the declaration block is required. An example of how this is done is given below:

<body style='color: white;'>
</body>

This HTML tag performs the same functionality as the CSS code specified in the previous section. The advantage of using this approach is that the style information given in this manner overwrites any other styling information. Therefore, if you need to use different style for one element while the rest of the document needs to follow a different style, then you can use a stylesheet for the document and specify the style for this element in its tag.

How to Use Embedded Style

Another approach for accomplishing the same outcome as inline styles is to use the <style> element within the element concerned, for defining its style specification. Here is how this can be done:

```
<!DOCTYPE html>
<html xmlns='http://www.w3.org/1999/xhtml'>
<head>
<title></title>
<style>
body {
color: white;
}
</style>
</head>
<body>
</body>
</html>
```

How to Create External Style Sheet

For usages where you wish to use the same style for the complete webpage or a number of webpages, the best approach is to use an external style sheet.

This external style sheet can be linked to the HTML page in the following manner:

```
<!DOCTYPE html>
<html xmlns='http://www.w3.org/1999/xhtml'>
<head>
<title></title>
<link          rel='stylesheet'          type='text/css' href='Content/mainstyle.css' />
</head>
<body>
</body>
```

</html>

You must create a file mainstyle.css, in the Content folder, and put the style rule specified below into the file.

body {

color: white;

}

Defining Media

It is important to note that a style sheet can contain as many style rules as you want. Besides this, you can also link different CSS files for different media. The different media types are as follows:

- all
- embossed

- braille
- print
- handheld
- speech
- screen
- tv
- tty

The media used can be defined in the following manner:

<link rel='stylesheet' type='text/css' href='Content/all.css' media='all' />

Defining Character Encoding

You can also define the character encoding used, using the following format:

Style sheet:

Place the following line above the style rule in the style sheet.

@charset 'UTF-8';

HTML page:

You must place this line above the link element.

<meta http-equiv='Content-Type' content='text/html;charset=UTF-8' >

Importing style Sheets

As your web pages becomes complex, the style sheets used shall also grow in complexity. Therefore, you may need to use many style sheets. You can import the style rules present in one style sheet to another by using:

@import url('/Content/header.css');

Here, header.css is imported and the url gives the relative address of the style sheet to be imported.

Importing Fonts

Fonts can be imported using the following format:

@font-face {

font-family: newFont;

src: url('New_Font.ttf'),

url('New_Font.eot'); /* IE9 */

Selectors, Specificity and Cascading

Selectors can be of three types, class selectors, ID selectors and element selectors. The element selector type is the simplest and requires you to simply name the element that needs to be used. For instance, if you wish to change the background color of the body, then the element selector used is *body*.

While declaring any element, you can assign an ID to it using the id attribute. You can use this ID prefixed with a # as a selector. For example, if you have created a button with ID btnID, then the ID selector for this will be #btnID. Similarly, you can assign a class name to an element using the class attribute. Class name can be used prefixed by a dot(.) in the following manner, .className.

However, if you wish to select all the elements of the webpage, then asterisk (*) to it.

Using Descendent and Child Selectors

You may wish to apply a particular style to a descendant of a selector. This can be done by specifying the complete selector change. It can be done in the following manner:

li a {

text-color: black;

}

On the other hand, you may want to apply to an element only if it is a direct child of the selector. This can be implemented by specifying the parent and child separated by a greater than (>) sign, in the following manner:

li > a {

color: white;

}

Pseudo-element and Pseudo-class Selectors

Now that you know how to apply styles to specific elements, let us move on to implementing styles to more specific sections like the first line of the second paragraph. In order to style elements that cannot be classified on the basis of name, content or is not a part of the DOM tree can be styled using pseudo-classes. The available pseudo-classes include:

- :visited
- :link
- :hover
- :active
- :checked
- :focus

- :nth-last-child(n)
- :not
- :only-child
- :nth-child(formula)
- :lang(language)
- :first-of-type
- :only-of-type

If you want to access information of the DOM tree that is not accessible otherwise, you can use pseudo-elements. Pseudo-elements include:

- ::first-letter
- ::first-line
- ::after
- ::before

Grouping Selectors

Multiple selectors can be used for a style rule. These selectors must be separated by commas. Sample implementation:

```
body, button {
color: white;
}
```

Using Adjacent Selectors

If you want to style the first heading in a div or any similar adjacent elements, the selector is constructed using a plus sign (+) between the two selectors. Sample implementation:

```
div + h1 {
color: white;
}
```

Sibling Selectors

Sibling selectors are similar to adjacent selectors except for the fact that all the matching elements are styled as against adjacent selectors, which only style the first matching element. The selector is constructed using a ~ sign between the two selectors. Sample implementation:

div ~ h1 {

color: white;

}

Using Attribute Selector

This selector selects all the elements for which the specified attribute exists. The selector is written in this form:

a[title]

This selector will select all the links for which the title attribute has been specified. Moreover, this selector type can be modified into attribute-value selector by specifying the attribute value in the following manner:

a[title = value]

In-Built Styles of Browsers

Every browser has a built-in stylesheet, which is applied to all the webpages opened using this browser. In fact, this stylesheet is applied before any other style sheet. You can define your own style sheet for the browser using the Accessibility option in Tools. However, user style sheets are browser specific. Therefore, if you open a different browser, the style sheet you defined may not be accessible.

In case, you want your user-defined stylesheet to override any other style specified in the HTML page, then you can use the '!important' modifier. This modifier sets highest priority for the specified style statement. Sample implementation:

body {

color: white !important;

}

Cascading of Styles

The precedence and priority of the styles are decided on the basis of the following parameters.

- Importance
- Specificity
- Textual Order

Working with CSS Properties

Now that you are thorough with the use of selectors, the next step is to look at CSS properties.

Color

One of the most crucial properties that are used in a web page is color, which can be defined using ARGB, RGB and color names.

RGB value are typically defined using a decimal number, which lies between 0-255.

- white #ffffff
- red #ff0000
- black #000000
- green #008000

Color values can also be used instead of the color name. An example of how this can be used is given below.

body {
color: #ffffff;
}

Another way to specify the color is using the RGB function, which specifies the values of parameters using a number between 0-255 or percentage. Example of this type of declaration is given below:

h1 { color: rgb(255,0,0); }

Other ways to specify color are RGBA, which accepts 4 values and HSL, which defines values for hue, saturation and lightness.

Transparency

The transparency or opacity are defined by a value between 0.0 (invisible) and 1.0 (opaque).

Text

As far as text is concerned, font-face and font-size can be specified. These properties can be defined in the following manner:

h1 { font-family: arial, verdana, sans-serif; }

h1 { font-size: 12px; }

The CSS Box Model

The CSS Box Model assumes that a webpage can be considered to be made up of boxes. The spacing between these boxes are given by margins and padding settings. These properties can be given values in the following manner:

margin: 15px;

padding: 25px;

border: 10px;

Positioning <div> elements

The element used for creating page layouts is <div>. Although, HTML5 recommends the use of semantic markup instead of div elements, there are still used for content that cannot be styled using semantic markup. A div element can be imagined as a rectangular block and is declared in the following manner:

<!—other elements are enclosed within this area-->

Properties used to define the position of a div element include:

- The position of the div element can be defined using the properties, top, bottom, left and right, in pixels.
- A property, position, is used to define if the position specified is static or relative.
- The float property can be used to allow elements to float to the right or left and is defined as float: left or float: right.
- The clear property places a clear element right after the floating element.
- You can also change the manner in which the browser calculates width with the help of the box-sizing property. This property can take three values: content-box (default setting), border-box and padding-box.

Centering Content

If you are using a fixed width, the div element can be centered using the properties, margin-left and margin-right. If you fix the width and set the margins to *auto,* the extra space on the margins is equally divided. It can be done in the following manner:

```
#container {
width: 850px;
margin-left: auto;
margin-right: auto;
}
```

5

HTML5 EXPLAINED

The chapter focuses on the basics of HTML5 and how they can be used for creating high performance, new-generation pages. However, most of the elements explained in that chapter included elements that HTML5 has received from its predecessors. This chapter takes you a step further in your quest of learning HTML5, introducing concepts that are newly added to this technology.

In the previous chapter on CSS, we introduced the concept of <div> element to you. This element is preferred over all its alternatives as far as page layout creation is concerned. While some people also use the <table> element, it is usually not a recommended solution as it is difficult to maintain as well use. However, both the concepts are elaborated upon this chapter.

Semantic Markup

The <div> and <span> elements are the most commonly used and recommended elements for positioning and formatting content. However, it is recommended that you should use different <div> elements for specifying different sections of the page like header and footer. This shall allow you to position them individually and in a more organized manner. Therefore, the W3C has named these new elements with names like <footer> and <header>.

Browser Support

It is true that your HTML code will not be read by any of your users. However, there are other tools and machines that are constantly parsing your code. These tools include web crawlers, which indexes webpages for searching and NVDA (Non-Visual Desktop Access) devices, which are used by many users with special needs as an alternative for reading and comprehending web pages. Therefore, they require you to use tags that are understandable.

How to Create HTML5 Documents

Although, the above discussion clearly mentions the importance of using meaning tags and prohibits the use of tags like <div> and <span>, you may still have to use them for styling purposes. As you read on, you will realize how semantic tags must be supplied for providing meaning to your tags. It is important to mention here that semantic tags should be used carefully, and if you realize that there is a need to define custom elements, then go ahead and use the <div> and <span> elements. However, be sure to add an ID and class-name to the elements that describe their meaning as well as possible.

How to Create HTML5 Layout Container

A layout container, as the name suggests, is a container that entails the layout of a page. In other words, the container contains the different sections of the layout or its children in such a manner that they can be positioned in a flexible manner. As a developer, you can easily distinguish between <div> elements on the basis of their class names and IDs. However, this is not true for browsers.

Therefore, there has got to be a way by which you can

ask the browser to interpret elements. For instance, you may want to ask the browser to focus on a certain <div> element upon opening. All this and more can be done with the help of layout containers that express elements in such a manner that they are understandable to both the browser and the user.

Some of the commonly used elements for creating a layout container include:

- *<header>*

It is used to define the header section or the topmost section of the HTML document. This element can also be defined inside the <article> element.

- *<footer>*

It is used to define the footer section or the bottom-most section of the HTML document. This element can also be defined inside the <article> element.

- *<nav>*

It is used to define the section that contains all the navigational links.

- *<aside>*

This element is generally used for sidebars and separates the content in the <aside> element from the content that is outside this element.

- *<section>*

This element defines a part of the whole section and is named with the elements <h1>, <h2>, <h3>, <h4>, <h5> and <h6>.

- *<article>*

This element defines a complete unit of content, which you can copy from one location to another. An example of such a unit is a blog post.

Using Roles

The role attribute can be declared inside the <div> and <aside> elements. The role class hierarchy and the usage of roles for providing specific meanings, as far as far as accessibility is concerned, is defined in WAI-ARIA (Web Accessible Initiative - Accessible Rich Internet Applications).

One of the parent role classes is the landmark role class, which defines the navigational landmarks on the webpage. The child classes of the parent role class include:

- banner

This defines website specific content that is not expected to change from one webpage to another like headers.

- application

This defines that the specified area is a web application.

- contentinfo

This defines the information included in the webpage

about the webpage like copyright information. This information is mostly a part of the footer content.

- complementary

This defines a section of the page that is meaningful when detached from the page as well.

- main

The main web page content is defined using this child role class.

- form

This defines the area of the webpage that is expected to take webpage inputs.

- search

This child role class is used to define the location on the webpage that is used for getting the search query from the user and displaying the results of the search.

- navigation

The area containing navigational links is a part of this child role class.

These roles can be used for providing meaning. However, the new elements included in HTML5 are meaningful themselves. Yet, there are some utilities that are not available in HTML5 and for these, role attribute can be used.

How to Control format using *<div>* element?

As mentioned previously, the <div> element is essentially invisible and does not provide any meaning to the element. However, if you wish to use it for formatting purposes only, then it is perfect for this purpose.

How to Add Thematic Breaks?

The void element <hr/> can be used for adding thematic breaks, which are used for denoting a transition from one set of content to another.

How to Annotate Content?

There are several elements available for annotation. These include <b> and <i>, which you have been using for ages. However, they have new meanings now, in addition to the style that they denote. For instance, the <b> element denotes the style 'bold'. In addition to this, HTML5 adds the meaning 'span of text with special focus, but no change in mood, importance level or implication.'

Although, the use of the bold style makes more sense in this context, but you can still use this element for denoting names of products in reviews or keywords. Similarly, the element <strong> indicates the relative importance of content and <i> denotes a change in mood or implication of the content concerned. Besides this, the <em> element is used for text that will be alternatively pronounced by the reader.

How to Use <abbr> for Acronyms and Abbreviations?

In the previous versions of HTML, the <acronym> element was used for this purpose. However, this element has become obsolete and the new element used for this purpose is <abbr>. It is an inline element, which is generally used with other inline elements like <em> and <strong>.

Element - <address>

This element is used for defining the contact information of the owner or the author of the webpage.

Quotations and Citations

You can indicate that a particular text is a quote by using the element <blackquote>, which is used for a long quotation, and <q>, which is used for an inline quotation. You can mention the source of the quotation using the cite attribute or the <cite> element. However, using the <cite> element inside <q> and <blackquote> elements is considered a better approach. Please remember that the <cite> element can only mention the name of the work and other information elements like author's name and location of publishing, are not included here.

How to Document Code in HTML5?

There are two elements, <code> and <samp>, are used for documenting code. While the element <code> is used for documenting the source code, the element <sample> is used for the output of the code. A sample HTML for how this is done is given below:

```
<code class="maintainWhiteSpace">
echoContent('Screen');
function echoContent(name)
{
alert('This is' + name + '.');
}
</code>
<samp class="maintainWhiteSpace">
This is Screen.
</samp>
```

The <pre> Element

It is important to mention here that these elements do not preserve the whitespace. Therefore, a class needs to be implemented for this purpose. This class should look like:

style rule.

.maintainWhiteSpace {

white-space: pre;

}

Some browsers may not support this style rule. Therefore, for such browsers, it is advisable to use the element <pre>. Therefore, <pre> element can be used for defining the pre-formatting rules.

The <var> Element

This element is used to declare that the text specified inside it, is a variable. Example:

<p>

The variable <var>i</var> represents the number of iterations for the loop to perform.

</p>

The *
* and *<wbr />* Elements

The <br/> element implements a line break. On the other hand, the <wbr/> implements a word break.

The <dfn> Element

There may be occasions when you wish to define a term. This can be done using the <dfn> element, which takes title as one of its attributes.

Working with Figures

Images and figures are an integral part of any web page content. Therefore, every figure can also be viewed as a unit of content, which may consist of a caption and a reference from the page to which it may belong. In order to define one or more images, the <figure> element is used. The element <figurecaption> can be used for defining the caption of the figure.

However, it is important to mention here that the <figure> element does not give any importance to the position of the figure and the same is included along with the content. However, if the position and location of the figure is of importance to you., then you must consider using the <div> element.

The <summary> and <details> Elements

The element <summary> contains the summary of the content of the webpage, which can be displayed in the form of a collapsible list using the <details> element. Therefore, when you load a page, only the contents of the <summary> element will be displayed, while the contents of the <details> element are displayed when the user clicks on the summary.

Other Annotations

In addition to the above mentioned, there are a few more annotations available, which include:

- *<s>* - Used for striking out text
- *<u>* - Used for underlining text
- *<mark>* - Used for highlighting text
- *<ins>* - Used for indicating that the text has been inserted
- *<del>* - Used for indicating that the text has been deleted
- *<small>* - used for indicating that the text must be printed in fine letters
- *<sub>* - Indicates that the text is a subscript
- *<sup>* - Indicates that the text is a superscript

- *<time>* - Used for indicating that the text denotes time and date
- *<kbd>* - used for indicating that the text is a user input

Language Elements

You may need to use characters of Chinese, Japanese or Korean origin in your text. In order to support this inclusion, the element <ruby> can be used. Inside this element, other elements like <bdi> and <bdo>, for defining the isolation and direction of text. Besides this, <rt> and <rp> elements can also be used for placing notation or parentheses in the text of <ruby> element.

Working with Lists

In HTML5, several elements for defining unordered, ordered and descriptive lists exist. A fourth category of 'Custom lists' is also present to allow customization by the developer. The list items for all these are declared using the <li> element. Moreover, all the three types of lists support list nesting.

Ordered Lists

Ordered lists are declared using the element <ol> and the elements of 'order' in this list are brought about by an automatic numbering of the elements that are included in this list. The attributes that can be used with ordered lists include:

- start - Used to set the starting number of the list
- reversed - Used for declaring if the list has to be ordered in an ascending or descending order
- type – Used for declaring the type of the list, which can be A, a, 1 or I.

Unordered Lists

This type of a list is declared using the <ul> element and there is no numbering of elements in this case. The elements of the lists are simply represented as bullet points.

Description Lists

This type of a list is declared using the <dl> element. Using this element, you can give a description containing zero or more terms. Besides this, the elements of the list are declared using the <dt> element, which specifies the term, and <dd>, which gives a description of the term.

Custom Lists

The developer can make use of CSS styles to create custom lists. In this case, a different style rule can be created for each level of a nested list.

Working with Tables

Another format for arranging and presenting data in webpages is tables. Tables are declared using the <table> element and represents data in a rows-columns format. The cells of the tables are defined using the <tr> and <td> elements. While <tr> is used for rows, <td> is used for columns.

Despite that fact that HTML5 tables are one of the most powerful constructs available to the developer, it is important to understand how and where tables can be most appropriately used. Here are the reasons why tables should not be used:

- The table created for a web page is not rendered until the </table> tag is read. On the other hand, if the same construct is created using the <div> element, the content will be rendered as it is read.

- Tables are extremely difficult to maintain.
- Tables are difficult to interpret for accessibility devices.

Sample Implementation:
```
<table>
<tr>
<td>Frank</td>
<td>1978</td>
</tr>
<tr>
<td>David</td>
<td>1967</td>
</tr>
<tr>
<td>Alex</td>
<td>1989</td></tr>
</table>
```
The table created above will look like:

Frank

1978

David

1967

Alex

1989

As you observe the table, you must have realized that the table is not complete unless we define what is called the table headers. This can be done using the <th> element. You can create table headers both vertically and horizontally. For example, we can define the following table header in the code used above.

```
<table>
<tr>
```

```
<th>Name</td>
<th>Year of Birth</td>
</tr>
<tr>
<td>Franky</td>
<td>1978</td>
</tr>
<tr>
<td>David</td>
<td>1967</td>
</tr>
<tr>
<td>Alex</td>
<td>1989</td></tr>
</table>
```

The resulting table for this code will look like this:

Name

Year of Birth

Franky

1978

David

1967

Alex

1989

In the above case, the table headers are simply of a larger font size. However, you can style these as you want by style rules. This can be done in the following manner:

```
th {
background-color: black;
color: white
}
```

This style rule will color the cells of the table headers with black color and the text will be written in white.

The normal behavior of most browsers is to automatically place all the <tr> elements in the <tbody>, indicating that this is the body of the table. However, it is a good practice to define the <tbody> explicitly. Besides this, the <thead> and <tfoot> can also be explicitly defined. The header, body and footer of the table can be individually styled using CSS. As a rule, you can have one header element, one or more body elements and one footer element.

The next important content feature that must be added to the table created above is the table caption. In order to define the table caption, the <caption> element is used.

In some cases, you may feel the need to style individual columns. This may seem like a difficult task considering the fact that tables are essentially row centric in HTML. While you have <tr> elements to identify rows, there are no <tc> elements for identifying columns. The <td> element identifies a cell. However, you can still style individual columns using the <colgroup> or <col> elements. The <table> element can have the <colgroup> element, which includes the <col> elements for columns that are a part of this group of elements. In addition, the <col> element also has a *span* attribute for defining the columns that are a part of this group. A sample implementation to explain how this works is given below:

```
<colgroup>
<col span="2" class="vHeader" />
</colgroup>
```

The CSS style rule for styling this group of columns can be something like this –

```
.vHeader {
color: red;
}
```

While the tables discussed till now are regular tables, HTML5 also supports irregular tables, which can be described as tables that have a different number of columns for each row. The rowspan and colspan attributes can be used for managing the layout of the table.

JAVASCRIPT AND JQUERY

You must have got a hang of the power of JavaScript already. In the chapter on JavaScript, you have already learnt how to create and adding JavaScript for making web pages dynamic. The biggest challenge of web development is to design webpage elements that can run just as well on any browser as different browsers provide support for different elements, making it difficult to find a common ground.

This chapter takes you a step further in JavaScript development by teaching you how to create objects and use them. Besides this, it also introduces you to the concept of jQuery, which attempts at creating browser-compatible code. Although, it cannot promise 100% browser compatibility, but it certainly solves the day-to-day issues regarding the same.

How to Create JavaScript Objects

Anything from numbers to strings are objects in Java-Script. Therefore, it is essential to know how to create and deal with these effectively. The simplest way to create objects in JavaScript is using the object literal syntax. The following example illustrates how it is done.

```
var customer 1 = {
yearOfBirth: 2000,
name: 'Alex',
getCustomerInfo: function () {
return 'Customer: ' + this.name + ' ' + this.yearOfBirth;
}
};
```

This code creates an object customer1, with the data members, name and yearOfBirth and the member function getCustomerInformation. It is also important to note the use of *this* keyword, which accesses the values correctly being used or referenced for the object concerned.

Besides this, you can also create objects dynamically using the new keyword. The methods inherited include:

- constructor
- isPrototypeOf
- hasOwnProperty
- toLocalString
- propertyIsEnumerable
- valueOf
- toString

Once the object has been created, properties can be added to the same in the following manner:

```
function getCustomer(myName, myYearOfBirth) {
var newCust = new Object();
newCust.name = myName;
newCust.yearOfBirth = myYearOfBirth;
newCust.getCustomerInfo = function () {
return 'Customer: ' + this.name + ' ' + this.yearOfBirth;
```

```
};
return newCust;
}
```

This code creates an object newCust dynamically. Several instances of this can be created in the following manner:

```
var cust1 = getCustomer ('Alex', 1978);
var cust2 = getCustomer ('David', 1986);
```

Although, JavaScript doesn't support a particular keyword 'class', but you can simulate classes using the method mentioned above.

Namespaces

There is no specific keyword like *namespace* for implementing namespaces. However, namespaces can be implemented using the concepts of classes and objects. If you classify variables and methods into objects and access them as instances of these objects, then you are placing only the names of these objects in the global namespace, reducing the scope of the variables to the object that they belong.

Implementing Inheritance

You can define 'is-a' relationships between objects in JavaScript by creating objects and then classifying those objects on the basis of their common characteristics. For instance, if you are implementing an object for employee of a company. You can create objects for specific types of objects like managerTechnical, managerGeneral, technical-Staff, recruitmentStaff and officeStaff and then classify them into objects, technicalStaff, which includes the objects managerTechnical and technicalStaff, and adminStaff, which includes the managerGeneral, recruitmentStaff and officeStaff. In a similar manner, new functions can also be defined.

Working with jQuery

JQuery is a library of browser-compatible helper functions, which you can use in your code to minimize the efforts required for typing, implementation and testing. These functions are essentially written in JavaScript. Therefore, you can also call jQuery, a JavaScript library.

The list of functionalities that are available in jQuery include:

- Attributes, which are a group of methods that can be used for getting and setting attributes of the DOM elements.
- Ajax, which is a group of methods that provide support for synchronous and asynchronous server calls.
- Core Methods are the fundamental jQuery functions.
- Callbacks object is an object provided for management of callbacks.
- Data Methods are methods that facilitate the creation of association between DOM elements and arbitrary data.
- CSS Methods are methods that can be used for getting and setting CSS-related properties.
- Dimensions are methods that can be used for accessing and manipulating the dimensions of DOM elements.
- Deferred object is an object that is capable of registering multiple callbacks while maintaining the data of state change and propagating the same from one callback to the next.
- Forms are methods that are used for controlling form-related controls.

- Traversing, this is a group of methods that provide support for traversing the DOM.
- Effects are methods that can be used for creating animations for your webpage. Events are methods used to perform event-based execution.
- Selectors are methods that can be used for accessing elements of DOM in CSS selectors.
- Offset are methods that are used to position the DOM elements.
- Utilities, which is a group of utility methods

Before getting to use jQuery, you will need to include it into your project. Once you have installed it and you are ready to use it to your project, the next step is to learn how to use it.

First things first, you need to reference the jQuery library on the webpage that needs to use it in the following manner:

```
<script   type="text/javascript"   src="Scripts/qunit.js">
</script>
<script src="Scripts/jquery-1.8.2.js"></script>
```

The next thing to know is that the jQuery code that you are hoping to use in your HTML page lies in the jQuery namespace, which has an alias $. Therefore, you can write either jQuery.jFeature or $.jFeature when referring to a feature of jQuery.

Before, you can start using it in your webpages, you will also need to change the default.js file as follows:

```
function initialize() {
txtInput = $('#txtInput');
txtResult = $('#txtResult');
clear();
```

}

This allows you to use jQuery and CSS selectors by matching them using their IDs.

Also, as you move ahead with coding using jQuery, remember to refresh the screen using Ctrl+F5 after making any changes as the browser may not be able to catch the JavaScript modification right away. Moreover, use jQuery objects as much as possible because the cross-browser compatibility that they offer.

A DOM object can be referenced from a jQuery wrapper in the following manner:

var domElement = $('#txtInput')[0];

Here is a simple code that checks if the element exists before referencing it.

var domElement;
if($('#txtInput').length > 0){
domElement = $('#txtInput')[0];
}

How to Create a jQuery wrapper for Referencing a DOM element

A jQuery wrapper can be created from a DOM element reference in the following manner:

var myDoc = $(document);
var inText = $(this).text();

The first statement assigns the wrapped object to the variable. On the other hand, the second statement wraps the object referenced using *this*.

How to Add Event Listeners

jQuery provides the .on method for subscribing to events. Besides this, you can unsubscribe using the .off method. These methods can be used in the following manner:

$('#btnSubmitInfo').on('click', onSubmit);

$('#btnSubmitInfo').off('click', onSubmit);

How to Trigger Event Handlers

JQuery provides triggers or the method, triggerHandler, for triggering event handlers or handler code execution. This can be done in the following manner:

$('#btnSubmitInfo').triggerHandler('click');

Initialization Code

You will often be faced with the requirement to run an initialization code upon the loading of an HTML document. You can do this using jQuery in the following manner:

```
<script>
$(document).ready(function () {
initializationFunction();
});
</script>
```

This can be placed at the bottom of the HTML document. It will call the initializationFunction.

7
_____

FORMS

In the previous chapters, you have already studied how HTML documents can be created and manipulated. Taking a lead from them, we can now move on to understanding forms, which is one of the most crucial and commonly used units of content in webpage development.

Simply, a form is a way in which data is collected and sent to a location where it can be processed, which is a server in most cases. However, since we are yet to discuss server side scripting, we will focus on sending the data to an email address. However, it is important to note that we do not recommend this practice and it is used only for understanding purposes.

Web Communications

Before moving to the working of forms, it is important to know some basics of HTTP. A typical web communication consists of the following activities:

1. When a user browses a webpage, a request for access to a web server resource is initiated by sending a GET HTTP request.

2. The request is processed by the server and sends a response to the browser using HTTP protocol.

3. The browser process the server response and presents it to the user in the form of a 'form'.

4. The user enters inputs to the form and upon hitting the submit or enter button, this data is sent to the server, using HTTP protocol again.

5. This data is again processed by the server and the server posts its response to the browser, which is displayed on the webpage.

Web Servers

Originally, web servers were designed to receive and process requests and send the results back to the browser using HTTP. Initially, when the web pages were simple, such web servers were able to process a good number of requests per unit time. There were no states involved as sending and receiving requests were as simple as opening a connection, transferring data and closing the connection.

The new age web servers are much more equipped that these simple web servers. The web servers of today implement what is called the 'keep alive' features, which ensures that the connection remains open for a definite period of time in which subsequent requests by the same browser to the server can be entertained.

Web Browsers

The web browser is a desktop application, which displays web pages and manages user interactions between the webpages and the server. The communication between the web servers and pages is established using technologies like AJAX and Asynchronous JavaScript.

How is Data Submitted to the Web Server

An HTML form can be created using the <form> element in the following manner:

<form method="post" action="getCustomerInformation.aspx" >

Enter Customer Number:

<input type="text" name="Number" />

<input type="submit" value="Get Customer Information" />

</form>

This form takes in the customer number and returns a page that displays the details of the customer.

However, it is important to note that not all elements can be used for submitting data in a form. The allowed elements for this purpose are:

- <textarea> - It takes a multi-line input
- <button> - It is a clickable button, which can be placed on any content or image.
- <select> - It is a drop-down list, which allows multiple selections. The selected options can be identified using jQuery: $('option:selected')
- <input type='checkbox'> - It is a checkbox, which has a value attribute used for setting as well as reading the status of the checkbox. The jQuery for identifying checked checkboxes is:
  $('input[type=checkbox]:checked')
- <input type='button'> - It is a clickable button, which has a text prompt.
- <input type='datetime'> - It is a control, which is date and time (UTC).
- <input type='date'> - It is a control, which is date-only.

- <input type='email'> - It is a file-select field, which has a browse button for uploading a file.
- <input type='color'> - It is a color picker.
- <input type='hidden'> - It is a hidden input field.
- <input type='datetime-local'> - It is a control, which is date and time (any timezone).
- <input type='month'> - It is a month-year control.
- <input type='image'> - It is an image submit button.
- <input type='password'> - It is a password field, with masked characters.
- <input type='number'> - It is a numeric field.
- <input type='range'> - It is a control, which accepts a numeric value and defines the allowed range of values.
- <input type='radio'> - It is an option button, which has a value attribute for setting and reading the status of the button. The jQuery used for identifying the marked radio buttons is $('input[type=radio]:checked')
- <input type='search'> - It is a text field, which is used for entering the search string.
- <input type='reset'> - It is a button that can be used for resetting the fields of a form.
- <input type='url'> - It is a URL field.
- <input type='tel'> - It is a telephone number field.
- <input type='submit'> - It is a submit button.
- <input type='time'> - It is a control, which accepts a time value.
- <input type='text'> - It is a single-line text field.

- <input type='week'> - It is a week-year control.

The *<label>* Element

It is the element that is used to convey the meaning of an element to the user. The text in this element is displayed inside the textbox, which is auto-removed when the user clicks on it. You can also specify the style of a label.

Specifying Parent Forms

There may be situations where the submission elements of a form may not lie inside the same construct. Therefore, gathering data, in this case, can be quite a challenge. In order to address this issue, HTML5 provides an attribute, id, which can be set for multiple form elements. This shall allow data collection from different form elements in one go.

How to Trigger Form Submission

Upon triggering, all the data collected from the submission elements of the form or forms of the same id is sent to the server using an HTTP method. The <input> element can be used for triggering form submission. Besides this, you can also use JavaScript for this purpose. In order to implement this, you must give an id to the concerned form, myFirstForm. The default.js file, which is linked to the HTML document, must contain the following code:

```
$(document).ready(function () {
$('#myFirstButton').on('click', submitMyFirstForm);
});
function submitMyFirstForm() {
$('#myFirstForm').submit();
}
```

If the method attribute of the form is not given any value, then it is set to a default GET. Moreover, the action attribute will also have a default value. Therefore, the button click will reference the page to same page. However, the URL will now include a QueryString, which is a combination of values selection or entered by the user. For instance, if the form requests the user to enter Customer ID and the user enters 1245, then the QueryString will be:

customerID=1245

This QueryString will be appended to the URL in the following manner:

Mywebpage.asp? customerID=1245

It is also important to mention here that the QueryString is URI encoded. Therefore, special characters are represented by specific values. For instance, a space is represented as '+' and exclamation mark (!) as '%21'. Name-value pair is represented as 'name=value' and name-value pairs are separated by '&'.

How to Serialize the Form

You can serialize the form using the jQuery serialize method. This can be done in the following manner:

var myFormData = $('#myFirstForm').serialize();

You can decode the URI-encoded string using the following:

var data = decodeURIComponent(myFormData);

Using Autofocus Attribute

By default, the focus is not set to any element of the form. However, you can set focus using the focus method, which can be implemented in the following manner:

$('input[name="firstName"]').focus();

However, you can also set autofocus in the following manner:

<input   type="text"   name="firstName" autofocus="autofocus"/>

How to Use Data Submission Constraints

A form can send data only if it satisfies the following constraints:

- Name attribute must be set.
- You must have set the value of form submission element.
- The <form> element must have its form submission element defined and form submission elements should not be disabled.
- If multiple submit buttons have in implemented, the values will be submitted only on the click of the activated submit button.
- Select the check boxes
- Select the Option buttons
- The <option> elements must have set <option> elements.
- If there is a file selection field, one of the fields must be selected.
- The declare attribute of the object elements must be set

Always remember that the reset buttons don't send any data and the form need not have an ID for its data to be sent.

How to Use POST or GET

There are two HTTP methods available for submitting data to the server. These methods are GET and POST. In the former case, the URL is appended with the QueryString. However, in case of the latter, the information is sent within the message body.

Form Validation

It is beneficial to understand that the root of all security issues in web application is user data. The moment you decide to open your application to user data and interactions, you are making your application vulnerable to security threats. Therefore, you need to validate any data that you receive before processing it to prevent any issues from cropping up. Validation can be provided at the browser or server end. However, server side validation is recommended as browser-level validation can be easily manipulated.

The simplest form of validation that you can implement is using the required attribute in the <select> element. You can set this attribute in the following manner:

<select name="dateOfBirth" required="required">

The validation error generated is browser dependent and each browser has a different method of communication to the user that a field is required for submission.

Besides this, the placeholder attribute is also available, which keep the prompt fixed on the unfilled field until a value for the same is provided by the user. It can be implemented in the following manner:

<input type="text" name="Date of birth" required="required" placeholder="enter the date of birth"/>

The addition of time, date and type based inputs in HTML5 makes validation much simpler as they can directly be matched to see if they have valid input values or not. Besides this, email, numbers and ranges can also be easily validated.

HTML5 performs validation and matches it with the :valid or :invalid pseudoclasses. If the validation is successful, the value is matched to :valid, else it is matched to :invalid. However, if a value is not 'required', it is matched to :optional pseudoclass.

WEB SERVICES

All the chapters discussed till now dealt with browser level coding and scripting. However, now it is time to move on to server side scripting. This chapter focuses on the use of JavaScript at the server level, which is possible with the help of Node.js, and how you can work around with web services.

Basics of Node.js

Node.js is a platform, which is made on Google Chrome, and can be used for creating scalable and flexible applications. It allows you to write JavaScript code for the server. However, before you can begin, you must download and install Node.js on your system.

Writing a Basic Code

The first step is to open any text editor and create a file named myFile.js. In the file, write the code:

```
var http = require('http');
http.createServer(function (request, response) {
response.writeHead(200, {'Content-Type': 'text/plain'});
response.end('Hello World!\n');
console.log('Handled request');
```

```
}).listen(8080, 'localhost');
console.log('Server running at http://localhost:8080/');
```

The first line loads the http module while the second line creates a server object. The function createServer takes in two parameters, request and response. All the website handling is done from these functions. In this example, the response function ends by writing 'Hello World' on the screen.

The function createServer, returns a server object, which call the function, listen. This function listens at the port 8080 and the IP address of the host is set to 127.0.0.1. therefore, if there is a network adapter installed on your system, your web server will start listening to web requests rights away. The last line prints a line on the screen to let the user know that the server is running and listening to requests.

Once you have created the file and saved the contents of the file as mentioned above, you must open the command prompt and write the command:

Node myFile.js

Now, keeping the command prompt active, you must open the web browser and type the address: http://localhost:8080/

As soon as the request is sent and a response is received, the same is communicated to the user using the console window. If you have been able to do this successfully, then you have just created your first node.js website. If you wish to stop the running of the code, you can just press Ctrl+C.

Now that you know how requests are received, it is time to look at how these requests are processed and responses are generated. You may need to use the *url* module for parsing the QueryString.

The code mentioned below shows how you can parse

the URL string and generate a response in accordance with it.

```
var http = require('http');
var url = require('url');
http.createServer(function (request, response) {
var url_parts = url.parse(request.url, true);
response.writeHead(200, {'Content-Type': 'text/plain'});
response.end('Hey ' + url_parts.query.name + '.\n');
console.log('Handled request from ' + url_parts.query.name);
}).listen(8080, 'localhost');
console.log('Server            is            running            at: http://localhost:8080/');
```

You can test the running of this code in the similar manner as the previous code.

How to Create Node.js Module

You can create modules by writing code in the form of functions and then, calling these modules from the main code.

```
var myHttp = require('http');
var myUrl = require('url');
function start(){
http.createServer(function (request, response) {
var url_parts = url.parse(request.url, true);
response.writeHead(200, {'Content-Type': 'text/plain'});
response.end('Hello ' + url_parts.query.name + '!\n');
console.log('Handled request from ' + url_parts.query.name);
}).listen(8080, 'localhost');
console.log('Server running at http://localhost:8080/');
}
exports.start = start;
```

when you save this piece of code in a file, a module is

created. This module can be used by other functions using the require function. For instance, if the file is saved as sample1.js, then the start() can be used in another function using:

var samplex = require('./sample1.js');

sample1.start();

How to Create a Node.js package

A collection of modules is referred to as an application. Once you have published your package, it can be installed and used. Consider for example, a package of different mathematical modules.

The root folder must have the following:

README.md

\packName

\lib

main.js

\bin

mod1.js

mod2.js

Creating Aggregate Module

You may wish to make only one object for the user to access. The user should be able to access all the modules of the package through this object. In order to accomplish this, a main.js module must be created in the bin folder that must define the modules to be included in the module.exports.

How to Create README.md File

The README.md file is a help file that can be used by the developer as a startup guide for using your package. The extension of this file is .md, which is a short form for markdown. This format gives readability to the text written in this file.

A sample file of this type is given below:

samplePackage package

====================

In samplePackage, the following functions are available:

- **add** Performs addition of two numbers and presents the result.

- **sub** Performs subtraction of one number from the other and presents the result.

How to Create package.json File

This file contains the metadata for the package and can be created manually using the command:

npm init

This command creates the file, which can later be edited. A sample file is given below:

```
{
"name": "sampleFile",
"version": "0.0.0",
"description": "This is a sample file ",
"main": "bin/main.js",
"scripts": {
"test": "echo \"This is a test file\" && exit 1"
},
"repository": "",
"keywords": [
"sample",
"example",
"add",
"sub"
],
"author": "XYZ",
"license": "ABC"
}
```

In addition to test scripts, you can also give git scripts, which are the best available source control managers.

How to Publish a Package

As mentioned previously, a package can be defined in terms of a folder structure. When you publish your package, you make it accessible to all users. In order to perform this operation, you must use the npm command, which is also the command used for searching and installing packages. However, you shall be required to create an account for yourself before publishing any of your packages using the command: npm adduser. After you enter the required information, your account is created. However, what this also means us that there is no validation required. Therefore, anyone can add code to the repository. Therefore, you should be careful while downloading and installing packages from the registry.

In order to publish a package, you simply need to go to the root directory of the package and enter the command npm publish in the command prompt.

How to Install and Use the Package

A package that is published can be downloaded and installed by any user. You simply need to go to the folder and give the command, npm install samplePackage. This installs the package locally. On the other hand, if you wish to install the package globally, you can give the command, npm install –g samplePackage. For a global installation, you will need to create a link from each application to the global install using the command, npm link samplePackage.

The route to a global install is a junction. You can get into the node_modules folder and back using the cd command. Once you are inside the folder, you can give the command: npm install contoso, to initiate an install. You can now write some code that uses the package. A sample is given below:

```
var samplePackage = require('samplePackage');
var finalResult = o;
```

```
console.log();
finalResult = samplePackage.add (5,10);
console.log('add (5,10) = ' + finalResult);
console.log();
result = samplePackage.sub (50,10);
console.log('sub(50,10) = ' + finalResult);
console.log();
console.log('done');
```

This code tests the modules of the package. You can execute the code using:

node main

The package can be uninstalled locally using:

npm uninstall samplePackage

However, if you wish to uninstall the package globally, you can do it using

npm uninstall -g samplePackage

How to Use Express

1. The first step is to install Node.js and create a sample for keeping all .js files and projects. Besides this, you must also install Express, which is a web application framework for Node.js development.
2. You can create a package using the following set of commands and instructions.
3. npm init
4. You can create myPackage.js file containing the following contents:

```
{
"name": "Sample",
"version": "0.0.0",
"description": "This is a sample website.",
```

```
"main": "main.js",
"scripts": {
"test": "echo \"Error: Test not specified\" && exit 1"
},
"repository": "",
"author": "XYZ",
"license": "BSD"
}
"private": true,
"dependencies": {
"express": "3.0.0"
}
}
```

In order to use the file in Express, dependencies have to be added. Moreover, if you do not define it to be private, you may get an error from the firewall of your computer as it tries to load the page.

1. Give the install command: npm install
2. You can use the command, npm ls, to see if the package is present in the registry.
3. You can create a simple application using the following set of instructions:
4. Create a file myApp.js and add the following to the file:

```
var express = require('express');
var app = express();
```

1. You can define the route using the myApp.Method() syntax.

```
app.get('/', function(request, response){
```

```
response.send('Hey World!');
});
```

The code mentioned above will send the response 'Hey World!' as and when a request is received.

1. The last section of code that must be added is for listening to the request. This code is as follows:

```
var port = 8080;
app.listen(port);
console.log('Listening on port: ' + port);
```

1. Once the file is complete, you can save it and run it using the command, node app. So, now if you open the browser and enter the address http://localhost:8080/, you will get the response *Hey World!*.
2. You can add webpages to applications by replacing the app.get statement with app.use(express.static(__dirname + '/public')); This will allow you to use the same code for a number of webpages. Sample implementation of this concept is given below:

```
<!DOCTYPE html>
<html xmlns="http://www.w3.org/1999/xhtml">
<head>
<title></title>
</head>
<body>
<form method="get" action="/submitHey">
```

Enter First Name: <input type="text" name="firstName" />

<input type="submit" value="Submit" />

</form>

</body>

</html>

Please note that the action attribute is set to /submit-Hey. In other words, this resource is called at the server for handling the data that is passed to it using the QueryString. The myApp.js file should contain the following:

```
var express = require('express');
var app = express();
app.use(express.static(__dirname + '/public'));
app.get('/SubmitHey', function (request, response) {
response.writeHead(200, { 'Content-Type': 'text/html' });
response.write('Hey ' + request.query.userName + '!<br />');
response.end('Enjoy.');
console.log('Handled request from ' + request.query.userName);
});
var port = 8080;
app.listen(port);
console.log('Listening on port: ' + port);
```

The app can be run in the manner mentioned above.

1. The *formidable* package can be used for posting back data. While the previous method used the GET method, this method uses the POST method.

2. To illustrate how it works, create an HTML as follows:

```
<!DOCTYPE html>
<html xmlns="http://www.w3.org/1999/xhtml">
<head>
<title></title>
</head>
<body>
<form method="post" action="/SubmitHeyPost">
Enter Name: <input type="text" name="firstName" />
<input type="submit" value="Submit" />
</form>
</body>
</html>
```

1. Now, in the command prompt, you need to a give a command for retrieving the formidable package, which is:

npm info formidable

1. You can also modify the package.jason file in the following manner:

```
{
"name": "HelloExpress",
"version": "0.0.0",
"description": "Sample Website",
"main": "index.js",
"scripts": {
"test": "echo \"Error: test not specified\" && exit 1"
},
"repository": "",
"author": "XYZ",
"license": "BSD",
```

```
"private": true,
"dependencies": {
"formidable": "1.x",
"express": "3.0.0"
}
}
```

1. Now you can install the *formidable* package by typing the following command into the command prompt:

```
npm install
```

This command installs the package locally. Therefore, you will need to add a line to myApp.js that allows the file to reference the package:

```
var formidable = require('formidable');
```

1. A sample myApp.js file shall look like this:

```
var express = require('express');
var app = express();
var formidable = require('formidable');
app.use('/forms', express.static(__dirname + '/public'));
app.post('/SubmitHeyPost', function (request, response)
{
    if (request.method.toLowerCase() == 'post') {
    var form = new formidable.IncomingForm();
    form.parse(request, function (err, fields) {
    response.writeHead(200, { 'Content-Type': 'text/html'
});
    response.write('Hey ' + fields.userName + '!<br />');
    response.end('Enjoy this POST.');
    console.log('Handled request from ' + fields.userName);
```

```
    });
    }
    });
    app.get('/SubmitHey', function (request, response) {
    response.writeHead(200, { 'Content-Type': 'text/html'
});
    response.write('Hey ' + request.query.userName + '!<br
/>');
    response.end('Enjoy. ');
    console.log('Handled   request   from   '   +   request.-
query.userName);
    });
    var port = 8080;
    app.listen(port);
    console.log('Listening on: ' + port + 'port');
```

1. You can now run the application in a similar
   manner as you did for the previous example.

Working with web services

One of the biggest drawbacks of a typical website
scenario is that the HTML page is repainted even if the
new page is the same as the previous page. This causes you
to lose bandwidth and resources. This drawback can be
addressed using web services, which can be used for
sending and receiving data, with the benefit that the
HTML page is not repainted. The technology used for
sending requests is AJAX or Asynchronous JavaScript and
XML. This technology allow you to perform the data
sending operation asynchronously.

Before moving any further, it is important to know the
basics of web services and how they can be used. A client
needs to communicate with the web server on a regular

basis and this communication is facilitated by the web service. In this case, the client can be anyone from a machine using the web service to the web service itself. Therefore, the client, regardless what it is, needs to create and send a request to the web service, and receive and parse the responses.

You must have heard of the term mashups, which is a term used to describe applications that pierce together web services. Two main classes of web services exist, which are arbitrary web services and REST or representational state transfer. While the set of operations are arbitrary in the first case, there exists a uniform operations set in the second.

Representational State Transfer (REST)

This framework uses the standard HTTP operations, which are mapped to its create, delete, update and retrieve operations. Moreover, REST does not focus on interacting with messages. Instead, its interactions are focused towards stateless resources. This is perhaps the reason why REST concept is known for creation of clean URLs. Examples of REST URLs include http://localhost:8080/Customers/2, which deletes a customer and http://localhost:8080/Vehicles?VIN=XYZ12, which is used to retrieve the information about a vehicle for which a parameter is passed using GET method.

Some firewalls may not allow the use of POST and GET methods. Therefore, it is advisable to use 'verb' in the QueryString. An example of how the URL will look like is:

http://localhost:8080/Vehicles?
verb=DELETE&VIN=XYZ987

The HTTP protocol also allows you to implement security using the HTTPS version. REST provides several benefits like easy connection, faster operation and lesser consumption of resources. However, many developers prefer to use JSON or (JavaScript Object Notation) because it is compact in size. Besides this, REST only supports GET and POST, which restricts its capabilities, Therefore, some developers switch to RESTFUL.

Arbitrary Web Services

This type of web services is also referred to as big web services. An example of such services is WCF or Windows Communication Foundation. Arbitrary web services expand their realm of operations by not mapping their operations to only aspects of the protocol. As a result, they provide more functionality, which include many security mechanisms and message routing.

This type of web services possess a typical interface format, which can be used by the client for reading and parsing information. As a result, the client can make calls to the service immediately. A common API format is the Web Services Description Language (WSDL). In case of arbitrary web services, the client must assemble its request with the help of a SOAP (Simple Object Access Protocol) message. This web service does not use the HTTP protocol and instead uses the TCP.

How to Create RESTful Web Service using Node.js

In the example mentioned previously, the sample-Package can be exposed as web service. The GET method can be used on the package and the operation is passed as a parameter. A good RESTful implementation of this package can look something like this:

http://localhost:8080/samplePackage?operation=add&x=1&y=5

How to Use AJAX to Call Web Service

Web services can be called asynchronously using

AJAX, which is in actuality a JavaScript. Instead of making a call to the server and repainting the HTML document, AJAX just calls back to the server. In this case, the screen is not repainted. A sample implementation is given below:

A MyPage.html can be created with the following code:

```
<!DOCTYPE html>
<html xmlns="http://www.w3.org/1999/xhtml">
<head>
<title></title>
<script type="text/javascript" src="/scripts/jquery-1.8.2.min.js"></script>
<script type="text/javascript" src="/scripts/default.js"></script>
</head>
<body>
<form id="myForm">
Enter Value of X:<input type="text" id="x" /><br />
Enter Value of Y:<input type="text" id="y" /><br />
Result of Operation: <span id="result"></span><br />
<button id="btnAdd" type="button">Add the Numbers</button>
</form>
</body>
</html>
```

The default.js file must be modified to contain the code required for processing these functions. Be sure to check the version of jQuery and whether it matches the version name that you have mentioned in your default.js file. The <form> element used here is only a means of arranging the format of data and the data is not actually sent via the form to the server. The JavaScript and jQuery access the data entered and perform the AJAX call.

How to Use XMLHttpRequest

The object that actually makes an AJAX call is XMLHttpRequest, which can be used for sending/receiving XML and other types of data. This object can be used in the following manner:

```
var xmlhttp=new XMLHttpRequest();
xmlhttp.open("GET","/add?x=50&y=1",false);
xmlhttp.send();
var xmlDoc=xmlhttp.responseXML;
```

The first line creates the object while the second line sets up the use of GET method with the specified QueryString and the use of 'false' indicates that the operation must be performed asynchronously. The next line sends the request and the last line sets the response to a variable, which can be later read and parsed for processing the response.

However, the output generated is JSON and not XML, therefore, the default.js file must be changed to:

```
$(document).ready(function () {
$('#btnAdd').on('click', addTwoNum)
});
function addTwoNum() {
var x = document.getElementById('x').value;
var y = document.getElementById('y').value;
var result = document.getElementById('finalResult');
var xmlhttp = new XMLHttpRequest();
xmlhttp.open("GET", "/add?x=" + x + "&y=" + y , false);
xmlhttp.send();
var jsonObject = JSON.parse(xmlhttp.response);
result.innerHTML = jsonObject.result;
}
```

The code extracts the x and y values from the <input> element for the same. After this, the XMLHttpObject is created and the open method is called using the QueryString. After the execution of the send function, the response string is parsed. In order to test the page, you can give the command:

node app

This command starts the web service, after which you can open the browser window with the link:

http://localhost:8080/SamplePage.html

this code is operational now. However, you may wish to perform the AJAX call in an asynchronous manner. For this, you must locate the open method and change the 'false' parameter to 'true'. Besides this, you will also be required to subscribe to *onreadystateschange* for managing asynchronous call. This can be implemented in the following manner:

```
function addTwoNum () {
var a = document.getElementById('a').value;
var b = document.getElementById('b').value;
var result = document.getElementById('finalResult');
var xmlhttp = new XMLHttpRequest();
xmlhttp.onreadystatechange = function () {
if (xmlhttp.readyState == 4 && xmlhttp.status == 200)
{
var jsonObject = JSON.parse(xmlhttp.response);
result.innerHTML = jsonObject.result;
}
}
xmlhttp.open("GET", "/add?a=" + a + "&b=" + b , true);
xmlhttp.send();
}
```

The codes for states are as follows:

- 0 - Uninitialized
- 1 - Loading

- 2 - Loaded
- 3 - Interactive
- 4 - Completed

If progress events are provided by the server, you can subscribe to the browser's progress event. Then, an event listener can be added to initiate the execution of the code when the event is triggered. This can be done in the following manner:

```
function addTwoNum () {
var a = document.getElementById('a').value;
var b = document.getElementById('b').value;
var                     finalResult                     =
document.getElementById('finalResult');
var xmlhttp = new XMLHttpRequest();
xmlhttp.onreadystatechange = function () {
if (xmlhttp.readyState == 4 && xmlhttp.status == 200)
{
var jsonObject = JSON.parse(xmlhttp.response);
result.innerHTML = jsonObject.result;
}
}
xmlhttp.addEventListener("progress", updateProgress,
false);
xmlhttp.open("GET", "/add?a=" + a + "&b=" + b ,
true);
xmlhttp.send();
}
function updateProgress(evt) {
if (evt.lengthComputable) {
var percentComplete = evt.loaded / evt.total;
//display the progress by outputting percentComplete
} else {
```

// You need to know the total size to compute the progress

```
}
}
```

You can also perform error handling by subscribing to the error event and the abort event. This can be done in the following manner:

```
function addTwoNum () {
var a = document.getElementById('a').value;
var b = document.getElementById('b').value;
var finalResult = document.getElementById('finalResult');
var xmlhttp = new XMLHttpRequest();
xmlhttp.onreadystatechange = function () {
if (xmlhttp.readyState == 4 && xmlhttp.status == 200) {

var jsonObject = JSON.parse(xmlhttp.response);
result.innerHTML = jsonObject.result;
}
}
xmlhttp.addEventListener("progress", updateProgress, false);
xmlhttp.addEventListener("error", failed, false);
xmlhttp.addEventListener("abort", canceled, false);
xmlhttp.open("GET", "/addition?x=" + x + "&y=" + y , true);
xmlhttp.send();
}
function transferFailed(evt) {
alert("An error occurred");
}
function canceled(evt) {
alert("canceled by the user");
```

}

It is also beneficial for you to know that different browsers implement and respond to objects in different manners. Therefore, it is advised that you must XMLHttp-Request as jQuery wrappers. The use of jQuery makes the code browser independent. The jQuery wrapper for AJAX call is $ajax(), which accepts an object as a parameter. The above code can be re-implemented in the following manner:

```
function addTwoNum () {
var a = $('#a').val();
var b = $('#b').val();
var data = { "a": a, "b": b };
$.ajax({
url: '/add',
data: data,
type: 'GET',
cache: false,
dataType: 'json',
success: function (data) {
$('#result').html(data.result);
}
});
}
```

The variable values are retrieved and supplied to the ajax call. The other properties and objects are set as shown. Another topic of concern is CORS, or Cross-Origin Resource Sharing, which is a way for allowing cross-site AJAX calls.

WEBSOCKET COMMUNICATIONS

There are scenarios that may require the establishment of two-way communication between the client and the server. A sample application that requires this form of communication is a chat application. This chapter gives an elaborative study of how web socket communication can be established and used.

Communicating by using WebSocket

Websocket communications are established using the WebSocket protocol, which uses the TCP connection for establishing a full-duplex communication pathway. The protocol has been standardized by the IETF (RFC 6455) and the working draft of the WebSocket API is in W3C.

This technology has replaced the concept of long polling. In this case, the client sends a request and keeps waiting for a response until a response is received. The benefit of this approach is that the connection remains open and as and when the data is available, it is immediately sent. However, the connection may be timed out and a re-establishment may be required.

Understanding WebSocket Protocol

The WebSocket protocol allows bi-directional connection establishment and is designed for implementation for web servers and clients. This technology only interacts with the handshake and is interpreted as a transition from the http to WebSocket. The frame of this protocol has no headers and an overhead of 2 bytes. It is a lightweight technology and its high performance allows communication of live content and games.

Defining WebSocket API

The heart of the WebSocket technology is WebSocket object. This object is defined on the window object and contains the following members:

- close
- WebSocket constructor
- binaryType
- send
- extensions
- bufferedAmount
- onerror
- url
- onclose
- onopen
- onmessage
- readyState
- protocol

How to Implement WebSocket Object

The WebSocket communication is based on TCP and thus, it operates on port number 80. You can use any HTML form for demonstration. The WebSocket url is of the ws:// and wss:// form. In order to implement this form, you need to create an object of the WebSocket API, which can then be configured using onopen, onclose, onerror and onmessage events. The default.js file must be modified in the following manner:

```
/// <reference path="_references.js" />
var wsUri = 'ws://echo.websocket.org/';
var webSocket;
$(document).ready(function () {
if (checkSupported()) {
connect();
$('#btnSend').click(doSend);
}
});
function writeOutput(message) {
var output = $("#divOutput");
output.html(output.html() + '<br />' + message);
}
function checkSupported() {
if (window.WebSocket) {
writeOutput('WebSocket is supported!');
return true;
}
else {
writeOutput('WebSockets is not supported');
$('#btnSend').attr('disabled', 'disabled');
return false;
}
}
function connect() {
webSocket = new WebSocket(wsUri);
webSocket.onopen = function (evt) { onOpen(evt) };
webSocket.onclose = function (evt) { onClose(evt) };
webSocket.onmessage = function (evt) { onMessage(evt)
};
```

```
webSocket.onerror = function (evt) { onError(evt) };
}
function doSend() {
if (webSocket.readyState != webSocket.OPEN)
{
writeOutput("NOT OPEN: " + $('#txtMessage').val());
return;
}
writeOutput("SENT: " + $('#txtMessage').val());
webSocket.send($('#txtMessage').val());
}
function onOpen(evt) {
writeOutput("CONNECTED");
}
function onClose(evt) {
writeOutput("DISCONNECTED");
}
function onMessage(evt) {
writeOutput('RESPONSE: ' + evt.data);
}
function onError(evt) {
writeOutput('ERROR: ' + evt.data);
}
```

When you create a WebSocket object, a connection to URI is automatically initiated. The function, connect, subscribes the object the events mentioned above. The message is sent using the doSend function. However, the readyState property of the object is checked before sending any message. The values of the property can be as follows:

- Closed = 3
- Closing = 2
- Open = 1

- Connecting = 0

Upon reception of message from the server, the client calls the onMessage function, which passes the event object. The property, data, of this object, contains the message sent from the server. On the contrary, if an error has occurred, then the onError function is called and the data property contains the reason for error generation. In some cases, the data property may be 'undefined'. This is particularly the case in scenarios where the connection has timed-out.

How to Deal with Timeouts

A timeout is identified when no activity is triggered for as long as 20 minutes. One of the most effective ways to deal with timeouts is sending an empty message to the server on a periodic basis. This can be done in the following manner.

```
/// <reference path="_references.js" />
var wsUri = 'ws://echo.websocket.org/';
var webSocket;
var timerId = 0;
$(document).ready(function () {
if (checkSupported()) {
connect();
$('#btnSend').click(doSend);
}
});
function writeOutput(message) {
var output = $("#divOutput");
output.html(output.html() + '<br />' + message);
}
function checkSupported() {
if (window.WebSocket) {
```

```
writeOutput('WebSockets supported!');
return true;
}
else {
writeOutput('WebSockets NOT supported');
$('#btnSend').attr('disabled', 'disabled');
return false;
}
}
function connect() {
webSocket = new WebSocket(wsUri);
webSocket.onopen = function (evt) { onOpen(evt) };
webSocket.onclose = function (evt) { onClose(evt) };
webSocket.onmessage = function (evt) { onMessage(evt)
};
webSocket.onerror = function (evt) { onError(evt) };
}
function keepAlive() {
var timeout = 15000;
if (webSocket.readyState == webSocket.OPEN) {
webSocket.send('');
}
timerId = setTimeout(keepAlive, timeout);
}
function cancelKeepAlive() {
if (timerId) {
cancelTimeout(timerId);
}
}
function doSend() {
if (webSocket.readyState != webSocket.OPEN)
{
writeOutput("NOT OPEN: " + $('#txtMessage').val());
```

```
return;
}
writeOutput("SENT: " + $('#txtMessage').val());
webSocket.send($('#txtMessage').val());
}
function onOpen(evt) {
writeOutput("CONNECTED");
keepAlive();
}
function onClose(evt) {
cancelKeepAlive();
writeOutput("DISCONNECTED");
}
function onMessage(evt) {
writeOutput('RESPONSE: ' + evt.data);
}
function onError(evt) {
writeOutput('ERROR: ' + evt.data);
}
```

How to Handle Disconnects

Connections may sometime close errors concerning the network. Therefore, you may be required to call the connect function while you are inside the construct of the onClose function. This may lead to issues. A common problem faced in this regard is that the server is unable to identify that this new connection request belongs to a client that already exists. You can handle this issue by sending an identification message to the server.

How to Deal with Web Farms

You may need to run your application in web farm, in which case the incoming requests may be handled by many servers. Multiple server are used to perform load balancing and performance optimization. In this case, you can implement sticky servers, which ensures that a client is served by only one server. In other words, all the requests by one client are processed by the same server. This helps you to address issues that may arise due to open connections. These problems can also be handled using products like Microsoft App Fabric Caching Service and Redis.

How to Use WebSocket Libraries

Dealing with all the issues mentioned above can be challenging. Therefore, the best way to deal with the situation is to use server and client libraries. There are several libraries like SignalR and Socket.IO are available for you to explore.

MANAGING LOCAL DATA WITH THE HELP OF WEB STORAGE

Most of the topics discussed in the previous section focused on improving the performance of the websites and the services that it provides its customers. Therefore, handling information or data has been restricted to the data that is transferred between the client and server. In such a case, the server needs to wait for the complete round trip to occur. This involves cost overheads.

In order to address this issue, most modern day browsers have started supporting web or DOM storage, which allows storage of some data at the client level. This chapter provides an overview of storage mechanisms used and how they can be used to improve the performance of the system in this regard.

Introduction to Web Storage

In most web application, a server side storage solution like SQL Database Server is implemented. This may be an attempt to kill a mosquito with a sword. You don't need such a huge storage solution as storing small bits of information at the browser level could have solved your purpose.

Http cookies has been the most preferred and

commonly used form of data storage at the browser level. In fact, it is used by most browsers for storing user information. The cookie value can be set in the following manner:

```
function        setCookieValue(cName,        cValue,
daysToExpire) {
var daysToExpire = new Date();
daysToExpire.setDate(daysToExpire.getDate() + days-
ToExpire);
cValue = cValue + "; expires=" + daysToExpire.to-
UTCString();
document.cookie = cName + "=" + cValue;
}
```

The cookie value can be retrieved using the following code:

```
function getCookieValue(cName)
{
var cookie = document.cookie.split(";");
for (var i = 0; i < cookie.length; i++) {
var cookies = cookie[i];
var indexVal = cookies.indexOf("=");
var keyVal = cookies.substr(0, index);
var actualVal = cookies.substr(index + 1);
if (keyVal == cName)
return actualVal;
}
}
```

The last segment of code, shown below, illustrates how cookies can be used.

```
setCookie('fName', Clark, 1);
var fName = getCookie('fName');
```

You can also use the cookie plug-in available in jQuery, which can be used in the following manner:

```
$.cookie('fName', 'Clark');
```

var fName = $.cookie('fName');

Although, cookies are extensively used, they pose some serious issues like overhead and capacity limitation. Some alternatives available include:

- Google Gears
- User Data
- Java Applets
- Flash Player

These options are better cookies and addresses its limitations, but they suffer from some issues, which include:

- Pug-in is required
- User can block them
- Not useful for corporate users
- They are vendor-specific.

HTML5 Storage

Although, these tools offers some good, yet potentially improvable solutions, HTML5 has come up with some innovative tools in their attempt to provide a comprehensive solution.

- **Web storage**

The simplest form of storing data over the web is web storage, in which key-value pairs are stored.

- **Web SQL database**

If the application requires a full relational database, then Web SQL database is also available for us.

- **IndexedDB**

This is a NoSQL database that is seen as a good alternative to its relational counterpart. It is considered to be a good option for complex database requirements.

- **Filesystem API**

This is the preferred form of data storage is the data is of larger data types like images, audios and videos.

In all of the above mentioned types of data storage, the data is tied to the URL. Therefore, this data cannot be accessed by other websites. This is an important consideration when multiple websites are hosted on a shared domain.

Exploring localStorage

LocalStorage is one of the two storage mechanisms used for data storage. It is basically a Storage Object, which is stored as a global variable. The biggest advantage of using this mechanism is that the API provided for reading and writing data is simple and easy to use.

How to Use localStorage Object Reference

The attributes and methods available include:

- **setItem(key, value)**

It is a method that is used to set a value with the help of an associated key. The syntax for this operation is:

localStorage.setItem('fName', $('#fName').val());

- **getItem(key)**

It is a method that is used to get a value associated to the specified key. The syntax for this operation is:

var fName = localStorage.getItem('fName');

If no value is set, then null is returned.

- **removeItem(key)**

It is a method that is used to remove a value associated to the specified key. The syntax for this operation is:

localStorage.removeItem('fName');

- **clear()**

Removes all items from the local storage. Its syntax is:

localStorage.clear();

- **length**

It is the property that returns the number of entries in the storage.

var count = localStorage.length;

- **key(index)**

This method is used for finding the key associated with the given value. The syntax for this operations is:

var keyValue = localStorage.key(1);

One of the biggest benefits of using this storage mechanism is that it is supported by most modern browsers, unlike other storage mechanisms, which are supported by only a few browsers. Although, this mechanism is supported by most web browsers, it is a good idea to check it before using it. If the first reference to this storage returns null, then it can be assumed that the storage mechanism is not supported. In addition to this, you can also use the construct given below for this purpose:

```
function isWSSupported() {
return 'localStorage' in window;
}
if (isWSSupported()) {
localStorage.setItem('fName', $('#fName').val());
}
```

In addition to this, you can also use the Modernizr java-script library for the checking purpose. It is worth mentioning here that this type of web storage allows 5MB of web storage, as against the 4KB of web storage allowed by cookies. When the storage space is exceeded, an exception for the same is thrown by the system.

Although, web storage allows storage of strings only, but you can also store complex objects with the help of JSON utility methods.

How to Use Short-term Persistence with *sessionStorage*

SessionStorage is also a Storage Object, with the same attributes and methods as localStorage. The only difference between the two storage mechanisms is that sessionStorage stores data for the session only. If the browser window is closed, the data will no longer be available for use.

Issues Related to sessionStorage and local-Storage

Some of the issues related to these two storage mechanisms include:

1. Simultaneous reading and writing of the hard drive.
2. Slow searching capabilities.
3. No support for transactions.

How to Handle Storage Events

Synchronization is the biggest challenge faced in the implementation of web storage. In order to deal with this issue, you can subscribe to storage events, which can notify you about any changes that may have been occurred. When you subscribe to a StorageEvent, you get access to the following properties:

- newValue
- oldValue
- url
- key
- storageArea

Unlike other events, cancelling or bubbling a StorageEvent is not allowed. You can subscribe to an event using the following construct:

function respond (exc) {
alert(exc.newValue);
}
window.addEventListener('storage', respond, false);

This event can be triggered using the following operation:

localStorage.setItem('name', Clark);

You can also bind to these events with the help of jQuery.

OFFLINE WEB APPLICATIONS

The previous chapter discussed storage, which is one of the most used offline application. However, in some scenarios, you may require better tools and advanced features like indexing, asynchronous support and handling transactions. These features are a part of the many other offline applications that are available.

This chapter discusses Websql and IndexedDB, which are relational constructs for data storage. However, they cannot be used for storing files. Therefore, FileSystem API is used for this purpose. The chapter ends with a discussion on how you can make your website offline-friendly using HTTP Cache.

Web SQL

Web SQL is a relational database and its most recent implementations are created on SQLite. However, it is important to mention that this database constrict is no longer supported by W3C yet it is still supported by many browsers.

How to Create and Open Database

A database can be created and opened using the

following syntax:

var dbase = openDatabase('Lib', '1.0', 'Sample library', 5 * 1024 * 1024);

The parameters are as follows:

- name
- version
- displayName
- estimatedSize
- creationCallback

How to Manipulate Database

Manipulation scripts in SQL can be given as parameter to the transaction.executeSql() function for manipulating the database. An example of how a table can be created is given below:

transaction.executeSql("CREATE TABLE IF NOT EXISTS employees(" +

"id INTEGER PRIMARY KEY AUTOIN-CREMENT," +

"fName TEXT,"+

"lName TEXT," +

)");

IndexedDB

Till now, you have dealt with the two extreme cases of storing data over the web. While the web storage mechanisms follows the simple key-value pair model, Web SQL is based on the relational database model. IndexedDB is an alternative model that lies somewhere in between these two models. It is capable of dealing with everything from strings to complex objects. However, while using this storage mechanism, use browser-independent methods.

A database can be opened or created in the following

manner:

```
var indexedDB = window.indexedDB;
var openRequest = indexedDB.open('Lib', 1);
```

An important facet of IndexedDB object is the keypath property, which is used to define the attributes that must be used as the key. If the specified property does not exist, then an auto-incrementing or auto-decrementing attribute can be created.

Indexes can be added using the following code:

```
var openRequest = indexedDB.open('Lib', 2);
openRequest.onupgradeneeded = function(response) {
var store = response.currentTarget.transaction.object-
Store("employees");
store.createIndex('lName', 'lName', { unique: false });
};
```

The parameters required are: Name, keypath and optional parameters. In a similar manner, indexes can be removed using the following code:

```
store.deleteIndex('lastName');
```

You can add and remove object stores storing the following code:

```
var openRequest = indexedDB.open('Lib', 3);
openRequest.onupgradeneeded = function(response) {
response.currentTarget.result.deleteObjectStore("employees");
};
```

Similarly, an object can be added in the following manner:

```
response.currentTarget.result.createObjectStore("em-
ployees", { keypath: 'email' });
```

The next set of operations include transactions, which are performed in the following manner:

1. A transaction has to be opened in the following

manner:

```
var    newTrans    =    dbase.transaction(['employees',
'payroll']);
```

1. You can add a new record in the following
   manner:

```
var openRequest = indexedDB.open('Lib', 1);
var dbase;
openRequest.onsuccess = function(response) {
dbase = openRequest.result;
addEmployee();
};
function addEmployee() {
var    myTrans    =    dbase.transaction('employees',
'readwrite');
var employees = myTrans.objectStore("employees");
var request = employees.add({fName: 'Sammy', lName:
'Carnie'});
request.onsuccess = function(response) {
alert('ID of New Record = ' + request.result);
};
request.onerror = function(response);
}
```

1. A record can be updated in the following
   manner:

```
var openRequest = indexedDB.open('Lib', 1);
var dbase;
openRequest.onsuccess = function(response) {
dbase = openRequest.result;
```

```
updateEmployee();
};
function updateEmployee() {
var    myTrans    =    dbase.transaction('employees',
'readwrite');
    var employees = myTrans.objectStore("employees");
    var request = employeess.put({fName: 'Sammy', lName:
'Carnie'}, 1);
    request.onsuccess = function(response) {
    alert('ID of Updated Record = ' + request.result);
    };
    request.onerror = function(response);
}
```

1. You can delete a record using the following
   code:

```
function deleteEmployee() {
var myTrans = dbase.transaction('authors', 'readwrite');
var employees = myTrans.objectStore("employees");
var request = employees.delete(1);
request.onsuccess = function(response);
request.onerror = function(response);
}
```

How to Work with FileSystem API

The above mentioned storage mechanisms can be used for storing data, which is in form of strings. However, complex data structures like files and images may also be stored using URIs. However, it is an excessively costly option. HTML5 offers a low cost and simpler option called FileSystem API for this purpose. Using this format, you can create files and directories on a user file system's sandboxed location.

The functionalities available include:

1. A FileSystem can be opened and created using:.

```
window.requestFileSystem(TEMPORARY, 5 * 1024 *
1024, getFile, handleError);
function getFile(fileSystem) {
fileSystem.root.getFile("sample.txt", { create: true }, file-
Opened, handleError);
}
function fileOpened(fileEntry) {
alert("File opened!");
}
function handleError(error) {
alert(error.code);
}
```

The parameters for the requestFileSystem() function are type, size, successCallback and errorCallback. On the other hand, the parameter for getFile() function are path and options.

1. You can write to a file using the following code:

```
function writeToFile(fileWriter) {
fileWriter.onwriteend = function() { alert('Success'); };
fileWriter.onerror = function() { alert('Failed'); };
fileWriter.write(new     Blob(['Hello     world'],     {type:
'text/plain'}));
}
```

You can append to a file using the following code:

```
function writeToFile(fileWriter) {
fileWriter.onwriteend = function() { alert('Success'); };
fileWriter.onerror = function() { alert('Failed'); };
```

```
fileWriter.seek(fileWriter.length);
fileWriter.write(new      Blob(['Hello      world'],      {type:
'text/plain'}));
}
```

1. You can read from a file using the following code:

```
function readFile(file) {
var fileReader = new FileReader();
fileReader.onloadend = function() { alert(this.result); };
fileReader.onerror = function() { alert('Failed'); };
fileReader.readAsText(file);
}
```

1. You can delete a file using the following code:

```
fileEntry.remove(fileRemoved, handleError);
```
Similar functions exist for directories as well.

Appendix

\<a\> Hyperlink

\<abbr\> Abbreviation

\<address\> Contact information

\<area\> Image map region

\<article\> Independent section

\<aside\> Auxiliary section

\<audio\> Audio stream

\<b\> Bold text

\<base\> Document base URI

\<bb\> Browser button

\<bdo\> Bi-directional text override

\<blockquote\> Long quotation

\<body> Main content
**\
** Line break
\<button> Push button control
\<canvas> Bitmap canvas
\<caption> Table caption
\<cite> Citation
\<code> Code fragment
\<col> Table column
\<colgroup> Table column group
\<command> Command that a user can invoke
\<datagrid> Interactive tree, list, or tabular data
\<datalist> Predefined control values
\<dd> Definition description
\<del> Deletion
\<details> Additional information
\<dfn> Defining instance of a term
\<dialog> Conversation
\<div> Generic division
\<dl> Description list
\<dt> Description term
\<em> Stress emphasis
\<embed> Embedded application
\<fieldset> Form control group
\<figure> A figure with a caption
\<footer> Section footer
\<form> Form
\<h1> Heading level 1
\<h2> Heading level 2
\<h3> Heading level 3
\<h4> Heading level 4
\<h5> Heading level 5

\<h6\> Heading level 6

\<head\> Document head

\<header\> Section header

\<hr\> Separator

\<html\> Document root

\<i\> Italic text

\<iframe\> Inline frame

\<img\> Image

\<input\> Form control

\<ins\> Insertion

\<kbd\> User input

\<label\> Form control label

\<legend\> Explanatory title or caption

\<li\> List item

\<link\> Link to resources

\<map\> Client-side image map

\<mark\> Marked or highlighted text

\<menu\> Command menu

\<meta\> Metadata

\<meter\> Scalar measurement

\<nav\> Navigation

\<noscript\> Alternative content for no script support

\<object\> Generic embedded resource

\<ol\> Ordered list

\<optgroup\> Option group

\<option\> Selection choice

\<output\> Output control

\<p\> Paragraph

\<param\> Plug-in parameter

\<pre\> Preformatted text

\<progress\> Progress of a task

\<q\> Inline quotation

\<rp\> Ruby parenthesis

\<rt\> Ruby text

\<ruby\> Ruby annotation

\<samp\> Sample output

\<script\> Linked or embedded script

\<section\> Document section

\<select\> Selection control

\<small\> Small print

\<source\> Media resource

\<span\> Generic inline container

\<strong\> Strong importance

\<style\> Embedded style sheet

\<sub\> Subscript

\<sup\> Superscript

\<table\> Table

\<tbody\> Table body

\<td\> Table cell

\<textarea\> Multiline text control

\<tfoot\> Table footer

\<th\> Table header cell

\<thead\> Table head

\<time\> Date and/or time

\<title\> Document title

\<tr\> Table row

\<ul\> Unordered list

\<var\> Variable

\<video\> Video or movie

\<wbr\> Optionally break up a large word at this element

SECTION 2: LEARN PHP & MYSQL

SECTION 2:
Learn PHP & MySQL

SCOTT SANDERSON

INTRODUCTION

PHP is presumably the most commonly used scripting language in the website development world. It is most often utilized to upgrade pages. With PHP, you can do things like make user credentials for login pages like password and username. In addition, you can create check points of interest from a structure, create discussions, picture displays, overviews, and a ton more features. In the event that you've run over a website page that is based on PHP, then the writer has composed some programming code to liven up the plain, old HTML.

PHP is known as a server-side programming language. That is on account of the fact that PHP doesn't get executed on your machine. In fact, it gets executed on the machine you asked the page from. The results are then given over to you, and showed in your program. Other scripting languages that you must have heard about include ASP, Python and Perl.

The most common clarification of simply what PHP remains for is "Hypertext Pre-processor". However, that would make it HPP, without a doubt? An optional clarification is that the initials originate from the most punctual form of the system, which was called Personal Home Page Tools. This is exactly where the letters "PHP" have been taken from.

Anyhow, PHP is popular to the point that in case you're searching for a profession in the website development or web scripting industry, then you simply need to know this. In these book, we'll get you up and running. What's more, assuredly, it will be a much simpler than you anticipate.

Beginning With PHP

Before you can compose and test your PHP scripts, there's one thing you'll require - a server! Luckily, you don't have to go out and purchase one. Actually, you won't be using any additional cash. That is the reason PHP is so successfully used on the commercial platform. But, since PHP is a server-side scripting language, you either need to get some web space with an organization that supports PHP, or make your machine imagine that it has a server. This is on the grounds of the fact that PHP is not running on your PC - it's executed on the server. The results are then sent once more to the customer PC (your machine).

Don't stress if this sounds a bit of overwhelming - we've run over a less demanding approach to get you up and running. We're going to be utilizing some product called Wampserver. This permits you to test your PHP scripts on isolated systems. It introduces all that you require, on the off chance that you have a Windows PC. We'll clarify how to get it introduced in a minute, and where to get it from. However, here is some quick advice for users of non-windows systems.

Apple Users

If you are an apple user, you can try the following links for setting up your system for running PHP.

http://www.onlamp.com/pub/a/mac/2001/12/07/apache.htm

in your attempts to get your system running smoothly, keep a stern check on the location of file storage and the address of localhost.

Linux Users

Secondly, if you work on a Linux system, then setting up your system for PHP can be tricky because there are a very few online resources available for your help. You can try your luck with the below mentioned links for some help.

Windows Users

Doing PHP programming is simpler for you if you are a Windows user, considering the fact that plenty of online help is just a click away. The first step for setting up your Wampserver is to download the software. You can search for it on Google and download it using the official website.

Assuredly, you have now downloaded Wampserver and are well acquainted with the software. This will provide for you a server at an isolated PC (Windows clients). So, now you are equipped enough to test your scripts. Assuming that you have the Wampserver setup with you, you can install it by following the instructions.

Once the main panel appears, look around the menu items for tabs for stopping and starting the server. Other links shall take you to document viewer and system help, in addition to other functionalities associated with the system. Click on localhost, and you'll see a page. Localhost simply alludes to the server running on your standalone machine. An alternate approach to allude to your server is by utilizing the IP address 127.0.0.1.

Your server should be up and running smoothly by now. If you are facing any issues, you can look for their solutions on online forums or seek expert help.

VARIABLES IN PHP

A variable is simply a stockpiling area. You place things into your stockpiling zones (variables) so you can utilize and control them within your projects. Things you generally need to store are numbers and content.

In case you're alright with the thought of variables, then you can proceed onward. If not, consider the following explanation. Assume you need to create a record of your attires. You hire two individuals to help you, a man and a lady. These two individuals are going to be your stockpiling zones. They are going to hold things for you, while you count up what you possess. The man and the lady, then, are variables.

You check what number of coats you have, and afterward offer these to the man. You tally what number of shoes you have, and offer these to the lady. Unfortunately, we have a terrible memory. The inquiry is, which one of your kin (variables) holds the layers and which one holds the shoes? To help you recollect that, you can give your kin names! You could call them something like this:

miss_shoes

mr_coats

Be that as it may, it's altogether up to you what names you give your kin (variables). On the off chance that you like, they could be called this:

boy_coats

girl_shoes

But since your memory is terrible, it's best to provide for them names that help you recollect what it is they are holding for you. There are a few things your kin shrug off being called. You can't start their names with an underscore (_), or a number. Anyhow most different characters are fine.

Alright, so your kins (variables) now have names. Be that as it may it's horrible simply providing for them a name. They are going to be doing some work for you, so you have to let them know what they will be doing. The man is going to be holding the coats. Anyhow we can detail what number of covers he will be holding. On the off chance that you have ten layers to provide for him, then you do the "telling" him this using the syntax shown below:

mr_coats = 10

In this way, the variable name starts things out, followed by an equivalent sign. After the equivalent sign, you tell your variable what it will be doing. Holding the number 10, for our situation. The equivalents sign, incidentally, is not so much an equivalent sign. It's called a task administrator. Anyway, don't stress over it, at this stage. Simply recall that you require the equivalents sign to store things in your variables.

Notwithstanding, you're learning PHP, so there's something missing. Two things, really. Initially, your kin (variables) require a dollar sign toward the starting (individuals are similar to that). So the actual statement should actually be similar to the statement given below.

$mr_coats = 10

In the event that you miss the dollar sign out, then your kin will decline to work! Yet the other thing missing is something truly particular and fastidious - a semi-colon. Lines of code in PHP need a semicolon toward the end, as shown in the statement below.

$mr_coats = 10;

In the event that you get any parse slips when you attempt to run your code, the first thing to check is whether you've missed the semicolon off the end. It simple to do, and can be disappointing. The following thing to check is whether you've passed up a major opportunity of finding a dollar sign. So the man is holding ten covers. We can do likewise thing with the other individual (variable) as well.

$miss_shoes = 20;

In this way, $miss_shoes is holding an estimation of 20. On the off chance that we then needed to include what number of things or items we have as such, we could set up another variable (Note the dollar sign at the beginning of the new variable):

$total_items

We can then include the covers and the shoes. So as to add in PHP, you can utilize a statement like the one shown below:

$total_items = $mr_coats + $miss_shoes;

Keep in mind, $mr_coats is holding an estimation of 10, and $miss_shoes is holding an estimation of 20. On the off chance that you utilize a plus sign for addition, PHP supposes that you need to add. So, it will work out the aggregate for you. The answer will then get put away in our new variable, the one we've called $total_items. A syntax equivalent of this statement is given below.

$total_items = 10 + 20;

Once more, PHP will see the addition sign and add the two together for you. Obviously, you can include more than two things to this addition formula.

$total_items = 10 + 20 + 9 + 50 + 1100;

Be that as it may, the thought is the same. PHP will see the addition signs and afterward include things up. The answer is then put away in your variable name, the one to the left of the equal sign.

Placing Text into PHP Variables

In the past segment, you perceived how to place numbers into variables. Be that as it may, you can likewise place content into your variables. Assume you need to know something about the coats or layering clothes that you possess. You can categorize our coats into categories like Winter layers, Coats or Summer layers. You can choose to index them, also. You can put immediate content into your variables. It a comparative approach to putting away numbers:

$coat_1 = " Summer Coats";

Once more, our variable name begins with a dollar sign ($). We've then provided for it the name coat_1. The 'equal to' sign takes after the variable name. After the sign, then again, we have content - Winter Coats. Anyhow, recognize the twofold quotes around our content. On the off chance that you don't encompass your content within quotes, you'll get unpredictable results. You can, in any case, use single quotes rather than twofold quotes, as shown in the statement below.

$coat_1 = Summer Coats';

Be that as it may you can't do this:

$coat\_1$ = Summer Coats";

In the above line, we've begun with a solitary quote and finished with a twofold quote. This will get you a mistake.

We can store other content in the same way:

$coat\_2$ = "Coats";

$coat\_3$ = "Winter Coats";

The content will then get put away in the variable to the left of the 'equal to' sign.

In this way, to recap, variables are zones, which possess a well-defined capacity. You utilize these capacity territories to control things like content and numbers. You'll be utilizing variables a great deal, and on the following few pages you'll perceive how they function in practice.

Using Variables With PHP

To begin with, we'll examine how to access what's in your variables. We're going to be reviewing our results on a site page. So check whether you can get this script working in the first place, in light of the fact that it's the one we'll be expanding on later in this chapter. Utilizing a content manager like your PHP programming or Notepad, can be helpful. You can duplicate and glue it, on the off chance that you lean toward. Anyway you take in more by writing it out yourself - it doesn't generally soak into your mind unless you're committing errors!

```
<html>
<head>
<title>Practicing Variables</title>
</head>
<body>
<?php print("It is working!"); ?>
</body>
</html>
```

When you are done with writing everything, finish by

saving the page as variable.php. At that point, simply run the script. Keep in mind: when you're saving your work, place it in the WWW organizer. To run the page, begin your program up and sort this in the location bar:

http://localhost/variable.php

On the off chance that you've made an organizer inside the www envelope, then the location to sort in your program would be something like:

http://localhost/Foldername/variable.php

Besides this, you ought to have seen the content "It is working!" showing up on as a result of your program. Assuming this is the case, Congratulations! You have a working server, which is up and running! In case you're utilizing Wampserver, you ought to see a symbol in the lowest part right of your screen. Click the symbol and select Start All Services from the menu of the task bar.

Out of the complete program, the line of importance is:

```
<?php print("It is working!"); ?>
```

Whatever is left of the script is out and out HTML code. How about we analyze the PHP in more detail. We've put the PHP in the BODY segment of a HTML page. Scripts can likewise, and frequently do, go in the HEAD area of a HTML page. You can likewise compose your script without any HTML. Anyway, before a program can perceive your script, it needs some assistance. You need to let it know what sort of script it is. Programs perceive PHP by searching for this accentuation (called syntax):

```
<?php ?>
```

So you require a left edge section (<) then an inquiry mark (?). After the inquiry imprint, write PHP (in upper or lowercase). After your script has completed, put an alternate inquiry mark. At last, you require a right plot section (

>). You can put to the extent that as you like between the opening and shutting sentence structure.

To show things on the page, we've utilized print( ). What you need the program to print goes between the round brackets. In case you're printing string content, then you require quotes (single or twofold quotes). To print what's within a variable, simply prefix the variable name with a dollar sign. At last, the line of code finishes as ordinary - with a semicolon (;).

Presently how about we adjust the essential page with the goal that we can set up a few variables. We'll attempt some content first. Keep the HTML as it may be, yet change your PHP from Code 1 to Code 2.

Code 1:

```
<?php print("It is working!"); ?>
```

Code 2:

```
<?php
print("it Worked!");
?>
```

Alright, it's a useless change! Anyhow, spreading your code out over more than one line makes it simpler to see and comprehend what you're doing. The present code only has a single line. In the following code, we have added some more code to the sample script.

```
<?php
$testing_string = "It is working!";
print("It is working!");
```

We've set up a variable called $testing_string. After the equivalents sign, the content "It is working!" has been included. The line is then finished with a semicolon. However, before running the script, you must add the following print line to the code:

```
print($testing_string);
```

At that point include a few comments

```php
<?php
/ -Variables in PHP Practice-
$testing_string = "It is working!";
print($testing_string);
?>
```

Comments in PHP are for your profit. They help you recall what the code should do. A comment can be included by writing two slices. This advises PHP to disregard whatever remains of the line. After the two slices, you can write anything you like. An alternate approach to include a comment makes use of the following format:

```
/* <comment
*/
```

Utilize this kind of commenting on the off chance that you need to overflow to more than one line. Whichever technique you pick, verify you add comments to your code: they truly do help. This is true particularly on the off chance that you need to send your code to another person!

How could you have been able to you get on? You ought to have seen that precisely the same content got printed to the page. Furthermore you may be supposing - what's the major ordeal? All things considered, what you simply did was to pass some content to a variable, and afterward have PHP print the data of the variable. It's an enormous step: your coding profession has now started!

You can join together coordinate content, and whatever is in your variable. The full stop (period or dab, to a few) is utilized for this. Assume you need to print out the following:

"My variable contains the estimation of 5". In PHP, you can do it using the code given below:

```php
<?php
```

```
$number_1 = 5;
$value_text = 'My variable contains the estimation of ';
print($value_text . $number_1);
?>
```

So now we have two variables. The new variable holds our string content. When we're printing the value of both variables, a full stop is utilized to distinguish the two. Go for the above script, and see what happens. Presently erase the dab and afterward attempt the code once more. Any lapses?

You can likewise do this kind of thing:

```
<?php
$number_1 = 5;
print ('My variable contains the estimation of " .
$number_1);
?>
```

This time, the immediate content is not inside a variable, yet recently included in the print explanation. Again a full stop is utilized to distinguish the string content from the variable name. What you've recently done is called linking or connecting. Attempt the new script and see what happens.

Addition

Alright, how about we do some adding with variables. To add in PHP, the addition operator or '+' sign is utilized. On the off chance that you have the code open from the previous section, take a stab at changing the full stop to an addition sign (+). Run the code, and see what happens.

To add the values of the variables, you simply separate every variable name with an in addition operator. Attempt this new script:

```
<?php
$number_1 = 4;
$number_2 = 3;
```

```
$sum_value = $number_1 + $number_2;
$value_text = 'Result = ';
print ($value_text . $sum_value);
?>
```

In the above script, we've included a second number, and doled out a value to it.

```
$number_2 = 3;
```

A third variable is then announced, which we've called $sum_value. To the right of the equivalents sign, we've included the value of the first variable and the value of the second variable:

```
$sum_value = $number_1 + $number_2;
```

PHP comprehends what is within the variables called $number_1 and $number_2, in light of the fact that we've quite recently let it know in the two lines above! It sees the addition operator, and then adds the two variable values together. It puts the response of the addition in the variable to the left of the equivalents sign (=), the one we've called $sum_value.

To print out the answer, we've utilized linking:

```
print ($value_text . $sum_value);
```

This script is somewhat more entangled than the ones you've been doing. In case you're a bit astounded, simply recollect what it is we're doing: adding the value of one variable to the same of an alternate. The critical line is this one:

```
$sum_value = $number_1 + $number_2;
```

The addition operation to the right of the equivalents sign gets computed first ($number_1 + $number_2). The aggregate of the operation is then put away in the variable to the left of the equivalents sign ($sum_value). You can, obviously, include more than two numbers.

Subtraction

We're not going to weigh things around subjecting you

to torrents of substantial Math! In any case you do need to know how to utilize the fundamental operators. First and foremost up is subtracting. Subtraction is pretty much the same as addition, which you did in the previous section. Rather than the addition sign (+), you need to utilize the minus sign (-). Change your $sum_value line to this, and run your code:

$sum_value = $number_1 - $number_2;

The $sum_value line is pretty much the same as the first. But we're currently utilizing the minus sign instead of the addition operator. When you run the script you ought to, obviously, get the answer 1. Once more, PHP recognizes what is within the variables called $number_1 and $number_2. It knows this in light of the fact that you relegated data values to these variables in the initial two lines.

At the point when PHP runs over the minus sign, it does the subtraction for you, and puts the answer into the variable on the left of the equivalents sign. We then utilize a print function to show what is within the variable. Much the same as addition, you can subtract more than one number at once. Attempt this:

```php
<?php
$number_1 = 3;
$number_2 = 4;
$number_3 = 30;
$sum_value = $number_3 - $number_2 - $number_1;
print ($sum_value);
?>
```

The answer you ought to get is 23. You can likewise blend addition operations with subtraction. Here's an illustration:

```php
<?php
$number_1 = 3;
```

```
$number_2 = 4;
$number_3 = 30;
$sum_value = $number_3 - $number_2 + $number_1;
print ($sum_value);
?>
```

Run the code above. What answer did you get? Is it true that it was the answer you were anticipating? Why do you think it printed the number it did? On the off chance that you thought it may have printed an alternate response to the one you got, the reason may be the way we set out the whole expression. Did we mean 30 - 4, and after that add 3? Alternately, did we mean add 3 and 4, and then subtract it from 30? The principal entirety would get 29, yet the second total would get 23.

To illuminate what you mean, you can utilize enclosures as a part of your wholes and parts of expressions. Here's the two separate forms of the expression. Attempt them both in your code. Be that as it may, note where the enclosures are:

Form one
```
$sum_value = ($number_3 - $number_2) + $number_1;
```
Form two
```
$sum_value = $number_3 - ($number_2 + $number_1);
```

It's generally a decent thought to utilize brackets within your holes, just to clear up what you need PHP to compute. That way, you won't get an exceptional answer!

An alternate motivation to utilize brackets is a direct result of something many refer to as operator precedence. In PHP, a few operators (particularly mathematical functions) are figured before others. This implies that you'll get answers that are totally surprising! Therefore, be sure to verify the order of execution of the operator used in an expression before anticipating any correct results.

Multiply

To multiply in PHP and pretty much every other programming language, the * operator is utilized. On the off chance that you see 3 * 4, it means duplicate 3 by 4. Here's some code for you to attempt:

```php
<?php
$number_1 = 10;
$number_2 = 20;
$sum_value = $number_2 * $number_1;
print ($sum_value);
?>
```

In the above code, we're simply multiplying whatever is within our two variables. We're then allotting the response to the variable on the left of the equivalents sign. You can most likely think about what the answer is without running the code! Much the same as subtraction and addition, you can multiply more than two numbers

Division

To divide one number by an alternate, the / operator is utilized within PHP. On the off chance that you see 25/5, it means isolate 5 into 25. Attempt it yourself using the code given below:

```php
<?php
$number_1 = 5;
$number_2 = 25;
$sum_value = $number_2/$number_1;
print ($sum_value);
?>
```

Once more, you must be watchful of operator precedence. Attempt this code:

```php
<?php
$number_1 = 5;
$number_2 = 25;
```

```
$number_3 = 10;
$sum_value = $number_3 - $number_2/$number_1;
print ($sum_value);
?>
```

PHP won't work out the entirety from left to right! Division is carried out before subtraction. So this will accomplish first:

```
$number_2/ $number_1
```

Also NOT this:

```
$number_3 - $number_2
```

Utilizing brackets will clear things up things and you will be able to perform the operations you want and get the correct results.

Working With Floating Point Numbers

A floating point number is one that has a speck in it, in the same way as 0.5 and 10.8. You needn't bother with any unique sentence structure to set these sorts of numbers up. Here's a case for you to attempt:

```
<?php
$number_1 = 3.6;
$number_2 = 1.4;
$sum_value = $number_2 + $number_1;
print ($sum_value);
?>
```

You can multiplication, subtraction, addition and division of numbers in precisely the same path as the whole numbers you've been utilizing. A cautioning accompanies the use of floating point numbers. You shouldn't believe them, in case you're after a ridiculously exact answer!

You saw in the last area that variables are capacity regions for your content and numbers. At the same time the reason you are putting away this data is with the goal that you can do something with them. On the off chance that you have put away a username in a variable, for instance, you'll then need to check if this is a legitimate username. To help you do the checking, something many refer to as Conditional Logic comes in as something exceptionally helpful. In the following segment, we'll investigate simply what Conditional Logic is and how it works.

CONDITIONAL LOGIC

Conditional Logic is about inquiring as to whether a condition is true or false and on the basis of the result of the condition evaluation, the corresponding code is executed. When you press a button named "Don't Press this Button – at any cost!" you are utilizing Conditional Logic. You are asking, "Admirably, what happens IF I do click the button?"

You utilize Conditional Logic as a part of your everyday life constantly:

"On the off chance that I turn the volume up on my stereo, will the neighbours be angry?"

"On the off chance that use all my cash on another pair of shoes, will it make me cheerful?"

"In the event that I study this course, will it enhance my site?"

Conditional Logic uses the "IF" word a considerable measure of times. Generally, you utilize Conditional Logic to test what is contained in a variable. You can then settle on choices focused around what is within the variable. As an illustration, contemplate the username once more. You may have a variable like this:

$username = "regular_visitor";

The content "regular_visitor" will then be put away within the variable called $username. You would utilize some Conditional Logic to test whether the variable $username truly does contain the name of one of your general guests. You need to ask:

"If $username is bona fide, then let $username have entry to the site."

In PHP, you utilize the "IF" word like this:

```
if ($username == "allowed") {
//Code to let client get to the site here;
}
```

Without any checking, the if articulation follows the following syntax:

```
if (<condition to be checked>) {
//Code
}
```

You can see it all the more plainly, here. To test a variable or condition, you begin with the saying "if". You then have a couple of round sections. You additionally require some more sections - wavy ones. You require the left wavy section first { and after that the right wavy section } toward the end of your if construct. Get them the wrong path round, and PHP declines to work. This will get you a lapse:

```
if($username == "allowed") }
//Code to Let client get to the site here
{
```

Along these lines, the following code can also be tested:

```
if($username == "allowed") {
/Code to Let client get to the site here;
{
```

The first has the wavy sections the wrong route round

(ought to be left then right), while the second one has two left wavy sections.

In the middle of the two round sections, you write the condition you need to test. In the illustration above, we're trying to see whether the variable called $username has an value, "allowed":

```
($username = "allowed")
```

Once more, you'll get a lapse in the event that you don't get your round sections right! So the language structure for the if proclamation is this:

```
if(testing_condition) {
//Code to be executed if the condition is true
}
```

In the event that you have to test two conditions identified with the same variable, if-else build can be utilized. The linguistic structure for the if else construct is this:

```
if (testing_condition) {
//code if condition is true
}
else {
//Code if condition is false
}
```

In the event that you take a gander at it closely, you'll see that you have an ordinary if Statement initially, which is followed by an "else" part. Here's the "else" part:

```
else {
//Code to be executed if the condition is false
}
```

Once more, the left and right wavy sections are utilized. You can likewise include "else if" parts to the if statements you've been investigating in the past segments. The syntax to be utilized for the purpose is given below:

```
else if (testing_condition) {
```

//Corresponding Code
}

Relational Operators

You saw in the last segment how to test what is within a variable. You utilized if, else ... if, and else. You also made use of the twofold equivalents sign (==) to test whether the variable was the same in value as the given condition. The twofold equivalents sign is known as a Comparison Operator. There a many of these "operands" that you can use for testing. Here's a rundown of the list of operators and what they can be used for. Investigate, and after that we'll see a couple of illustrations of how to utilize them.

Operator
Purpose
Syntax

==
Equal
a == b
!=
Not equal
a != b
>
Greater than
a > b
<
Lesser than
a < b
>=
Greater than or equal to
a >= b
<=
Lesser than or equal to

a <= b

Here's some more data on the above Operands.

== (Has the same value as)

The twofold equivalents sign can signify "Has an estimation of" or "Has the same value as". In the sample underneath, the variable called $variable_1 is continuously contrasted with the variable called $variable_2

if ($variable_1 == $variable_2) {
}

!= (Is NOT the same value as)

You can likewise test if one condition is NOT the same as an alternate. In this case, you require the shout imprint/equivalents sign mix (!=). In the event that you were trying for an authentic username, for instance, you could say:

if ($which_user_entered != $user_name) {
print("you're not a authenticated client of this site!");
}

The above code says, "If what the client entered is NOT the same as the quality in the variable got, $user_name, then print something out.

< (Less Than)

You'll need to test if one worth is short of what an alternate is. Utilize the left edge section for this (<)

> (Greater Than)

You'll additionally need to test if one worth is more than an alternate. Utilize the right point section for this (>)

<= (Less than or equivalents to)

For somewhat more accuracy, you can test to check whether one variable is short of or equivalent to an alternate. Utilize the left point section took after by the equivalents sign (<=)

>= *(Greater than or equivalents to)*

In the event that you have to test if one variable is more than or equivalent to an alternate, utilize the right point section took after by the equivalents sign (>=)

Switch – Case

For a real world conditional logic system, a long rundown of if and else ... if proclamations will be utilized. A superior alternative to this structure when testing a single variable is the Switch-Case construct. To perceive how switch case function, think about the accompanying code:

```php
<?php
$new_picture =tower;
switch ($new_picture) {
case 'dog':
print(Dog Picture');
break;
case 'tower':
print(Tower Picture');
break;
}
?>
```

In the code above, we put the string content "tower" into the variable called $new_picture. It's this content that we need to check. We need to comprehend what is within the variable, so we can show the right picture.

To test a solitary variable with a Switch Statement, the accompanying language structure is utilized:

```php
switch ($name_of_variable) {
case 'testing_value':
//code
break;
}
```

It looks a bit complex, so we'll separate it.

switch ($name_of_variable) {

You Start with the expression "switch" then a couple of round sections. Within the round brackets, you write the name of the variable you need to check. After the round sections, you require a left wavy bracket.

case 'testing_value':

The expression "case" is utilized before each one quality you need to check for. In our code, a rundown of qualities was originating from a drop-down menu. These quality were: tower and dog, among others. These are the qualities we require after the statement 'case'. After the content or variable you need to check for, a colon is required (:).

//code here

After the colon on the "case" line, you write the code you need to execute. Evidently, you'll get a mistake in the event that you pass up the opportunity of adding any semi-colons toward the end of your lines of code!

break;

You have to advise PHP to "Break out" of the switch explanation. In the event that you don't, PHP will basically drop down to the following case and execute every case that follows the matched case. Utilize the expression "break" to escape from the switch articulation.

In the event that you take a gander at the last few lines of the Switch Statement in this document, you'll see something else also that you can add to your code:

default:

print ("No Image Selected");

The default alternative is similar to the else from if ... else. It's utilized when there could be other, obscure, alternatives. A kind of "get all" alternative.

Logical Operators

And also the PHP correlation administrators you saw prior, there's likewise something many refer to as Logical Operators. You commonly utilize these when you need to test more than one condition at once. Case in point, you could verify whether the username and secret key are right from the same If Statement. Here's the table of these Operands.

Operator
Purpose
Usage
&&
Both condition should be true
a && b
||
One or both of the conditions should be true
a || b
AND
Both conditions are true
a AND b
XOR
Only one of the conditions is true
a XOR b
OR
One or both conditions are true
a OR b
!
Negation
!a

The new Operands are fairly unusual, in case you're reaching them with confusion. A few of them even do likewise thing! They are extremely helpful, however, so here's a more intensive look.

The && Operator

The && operator mean AND. Utilize this on the off chance that you require both conditions to be valid, as in our username and password testing. Truth be told, you would prefer not to give individuals access on the off chance that they simply get the username right or just the right password. Here's a sample code to illustrate the concept:

```
$user_name = 'registered_user';
$pass_word ='secret_password';
if ($user_name =='registered_user' && $pass_word =='secret_password') {
print("Welcome User!");
}
else {
print("Invalid username/password!");
}
```

The if explanation is used in the same manner as before. However, perceive that now two conditions are continuously tried:

```
$user_name == 'registered_user' && $pass_word =='secret_password'
```

This says, "If username is right AND the secret key is right, as well, then give the user access." Both conditions need to go between the round sections of your if proclamation.

The | Operator

The two straight lines mean OR. Utilize this operator when you just need one of your conditions to be true. For instance, assume you need to allow a markdown to individuals in the event that they have used more than 500 pounds OR they have an extraordinary key. Else they don't get any rebate. You'd then code like this:

```
$total_expenditure =500;
```

```
$special_coupon_key ='98765';
if ($total_spent == 500 | $special_coupon_key ==
'98765') {
    print("Discount applies!");
}
else {
    print("No discount!");
}
```

This time we're trying two conditions and just need ONE of them to return a true value. In the event that both of them are true, the code gets executed. On the off chance that they are both false, then PHP will proceed onward.

AND and OR

These are the same as && and || operators, discussed in the previous sections. However, there is an unobtrusive contrast. As a novice, you can just use the following format for implementing AND:

```
$USER_NAME == 'REGISTERED_USER' && $pass_-
word =='secret_password'
```

The following statement also means the same as:

$user_name == 'registered_user' AND $pass_word =='secret_password'

Which one you use is dependent upon your preference. AND is a ton simpler to peruse than &&. Similarly, OR is a great deal less demanding to peruse than ||. The distinction, by the way, is to do with Operator Precedence. We touched on this when we examined variables, prior. It shall be discussed in detail in the sections to follow

XOR

You likely won't require this one excessively. Anyway, its

utilized when you need to test if one estimation of two is genuine however NOT both. On the off chance that both conditions are the same, then PHP sees the declaration as false. On the off chance that they are both diverse, then the answer is true. Assume you needed to pick a victor between two hopefuls. Stand out of them can win. It's a XOR circumstance!

```
$contestant_1 = true;
$contestant_2 = true;
if($contestant_1 XOR $contestant_2) {
print("There can be only one winner!");
}
else {
print("Both cannot be winners!");
}
```

Check whether you can figure which of the two will print out, before running the script.

The ! Operator

This is known as the NOT operator. You utilize it to test whether something is NOT something else. You can likewise utilize it to turn around or negate the value of a true or false value. For instance, if you need to reset a variable to true, on the off chance that it's been set to false, and the other way around, you can use this operator for best results. Here's some code to attempt:

```
$not_value = false;
if($not_value == false) {
print(!$not_value);
}
```

The code above will print out the number 1. You'll see why when we handle Boolean values underneath. What we're stating here is, "If $test_value is false then the code must print what its NOT." What its NOT is true, so it will now get this quality. A bit confounded? It's a dubious one. However, it can prove to be useful!

Boolean Values

A Boolean value is one that can hold one of the following states: true and false. True is typically given an estimation of 1, and False is given an estimation of zero. You set them up much the same as different variables:

```
$t_value = 1;
$f_value = 0;
```

You can supplant the 1 and 0 with the words "true" and "false" (without the quotes). Yet a note of alert, in the event that you do. Attempt this script out, and see what happens:

```
<?php
$f_value = false;
$t_value = true;
print (" f_value = " . $f_value);
print ("t_value = " . $t_value);
?>
```

What you ought to discover is that the t_value will print "1", however the f_value won't print anything. Presently, supplant true with 1 and false with 0, in the script above, and see what prints out. Boolean values are extremely normal in programming, and you regularly see this kind of coding:

```
$t_value = true;
if ($true_value) {
print("True Value");
}
```

This is a shorthand method for saying "if $t_value holds a Boolean estimation of 1 then the print statement must be executed". This is the same as:

```
if ($t_value == 1) {
print("True");
```

```
}
```

The NOT operand is additionally utilized a great deal with this sort of if articulation:

```
$t_value = true;
if (!$t_value) {
print("True");
}
else {
print("False");
}
```

You'll likely meet Boolean values a great deal, amid your programming life. It's better to get a hang of them!

Operator Precedence

Here's a rundown of the operators you've met as such, and the request of priority. This can have any kind of effect, as we saw amid the numerical computations. Don't stress over these excessively, unless you're persuaded that your math or coherent is right. In which case, you may need to counsel the accompanying:

The main operators you haven't yet met on the rundown above are the = and != operators.

In late releases of PHP, two new operators have been presented: the triple equivalents sign (=) and a twofold equivalent (!=). These are utilized to test if one variable has the same value as an alternate AND the two are of the same type. A case would be:

```
$number_val = 2;
$text_val = 'two';
if ($number_val === $text_val) {
print("Both are same!");
}
else {
print("They are different!");
```

}

So this asks, "Do the variables match precisely?" Since one is content and the other is a number, the answer is "no", or false. We won't be utilizing these administrators much, but it always beneficial to know the options you have with you.

The operator precedence is as follows (highest priority to lowest priority):

- / % *
- - + .
- > >= < <=
- !== ===
- &&
- II
- AND
- OR
- XOR
- OR

PHP AND HTML FORMS

On the off chance that you know a little HTML, you will realize that the FORM labels can be utilized to interact with your clients. Things that can be added to a structure in the form of radio buttons, text boxes, drop down menus, checkboxes and submit buttons. A fundamental HTML structure with a text box and a submit button can be created in the following manner:

```
<html>
<head>
<title>a BASIC Form in HTML</title>
</head>
<body>
<form NAME ="form_1" METHOD =" " ACTION =
"">
<input TYPE = "text" VALUE ="user_credentials">
<input TYPE = "Submit" Name = "Submit_1" VALUE
= "Login_value">
</Form>
</body>
</html>
```

We won't clarify what all the HTML components do, as this is a book on PHP. Some commonality with the above is expected. Yet, we'll examine the METHOD, ACTION and SUBMIT properties in the structure above, in light of the fact that they are imperative.

In the event that a client goes to your site and needs to login, for instance, then you'll have to get the subtle elements from textboxes. When you have the text that the client entered, you then test it against a list of your clients. This list of clients is normally put away on a database, which we'll perceive how to code for in a later section. To start with, you have to think about the HTML properties METHOD, ACTION and SUBMIT.

METHOD Attribute

On the off chance that you take a gander at the first line of our structure from the last section, you'll perceive the use of an attribute called METHOD:

<form NAME ="form_1" METHOD =" " ACTION = "">

The Method ascribe is utilized to tell the program how the data ought to be sent. The two most well known techniques you can utilize are GET and POST. In any case our METHOD is clear. So transform it to this:

<form NAME ="form_1" METHOD ="get" ACTION = "">

To see what impact utilizing GET has, save your work again and after that click Submit on your form. The thing to recognize here is the location bar. The address would have been appended by the following string:

?Submit_1=login_value

This is an outcome of utilizing the GET system. The information from the structure winds up in the location bar. You'll see an inquiry imprint, emulated by information.

Submit_1 was the NAME of the button on the form, and Login_value was the VALUE of the button. This is what is returned by the GET technique. You utilize the GET system when the information you need returned is not pivotal data that needs securing. You can likewise utilize POST as the Method, rather than GET. Read underneath to see the distinction.

POST Attribute

In the past section, you saw what happened in the program's location bar when you utilized the GET technique for Form information. The option to GET is to utilize POST. Change the first line of your FORM to this:

<form NAME ="form_1" METHOD ="post" ACTION = "">

Shut your program down, and open it again. Load your page once more, and after that click the button. Your location bar will then resemble this not have the ? Submit1=login part anymore. That is on account of how we utilized POST as the strategy. Utilizing POST implies that the structure information won't get affixed to the location in the location bar for all to see.

We'll utilize both POST and GET all through the book. Be that as it may, it relies on upon the undertaking. If the information is not delicate then utilize GET, overall utilization POST. An alternate paramount quality of the Form tag is Action. Without Action, your structures won't go anyplace! We'll perceive how this works in the following part.

ACTION Attribute

The Action property is an essential attribute of your form. That is to say, "Where do you need the structure sent?". On the off chance that you miss it out, your structure won't go anyplace. You can send the structure information to an alternate PHP script, the same PHP script, an email address, a CGI script, or some other manifestation of script.

In PHP, a prominent strategy is to send the script to the same page that the structure is on – send it to itself, as such. So you have to change the structure of the form that you have been using until now. Place the accompanying, and change the ACTION line to this:

<form Name ="form_1" Method ="post" ACTION = "next_page.php">

So we're going to be sending the structure information to precisely the same page as the one we have stacked – to itself. We'll put some PHP on the page to handle the structure information. Anyway for the present, save your work again and after that click on submit. You won't see anything diverse, yet you shouldn't see any slip message either! When your script has an Action attribute set, you can then Submit it. Which we'll see in the following part.

SUBMIT Button

The HTML Submit is utilized to submit information to the script specified in ACTION. Sample code to illustrate how this works is given below:

<form Name ="form_1" Method ="post" ACTION = "next_page.php">

So the page specified in the ACTION quality is next_-page.php. To Submit this script, you require a HTML Submit button:

<input TYPE = "Submit" Name = "Submit_1" VALUE = "Login_value">

You don't have to do anything uncommon with a Submit. All the submitting is carried out. If the length of SUBMIT has an ACTION set, then your information will be sent to some place. In any case the NAME characteristic of the Submit comes in as something exceptionally helpful.

You can utilize this Name to test if the structure was truly submitted, or if the client recently clicked the refresh button.

This is critical when the PHP script is in agreement with the HTML structure. Our Submit is called "Submit_1", yet you can call it just about anything you like. Since you know all about METHOD, ACTION, and SUBMIT now, we can proceed onward to preparing the information that the client entered. To begin with, we shall explore how to get text entered by the user in the next section.

Text Boxes

You already know about METHOD and ACTIOn attributes by now. The METHOD characteristic lets you know how information is constantly sent, and the ACTION trait lets you know where it is to be sent. To get at the content that a client entered into a text area, the text box needs a NAME trait. You then tell PHP the NAME of the textbox you need to work with. Our text box hasn't got a NAME yet, so change your HTML to this:

<input TYPE = "text" VALUE ="username" NAME = "user_name">

The NAME of our textbox is user_name. It's this name that we will be utilizing as a part of a PHP script. To return information from a HTML structure, you utilize the accompanying statement:

$_post['element_name'];

You can appoint this to a variable:

$variable_name = $_post['element_name'];

Before we clarify all the language structure, add the accompanying PHP script to the HTML code you have. Make a point to include it the HEAD area of your HTML:

<html>
<head>

```
<title> My First HTML Form</title>
<?php
$my_user_name = $_post['user_name'];
print ($my_user_name);
?>
</head>
```

Save your work once more, and click the submit button to run your script. You ought to see this show up over your text box:

Erase the text "user_name" from the textbox, and click the button once more. Your new text ought to show up over the textbox. The content box itself, nonetheless, will in any case have "user_name" in it. This is on the grounds that the text box is getting reset when the information is come back to the program. The Value of the text box is what is continuously shown.

So how can it function?

The $_post[ ] is an inbuilt capacity you can use to get POST information from a structure. In the event that you had METHOD = "GET" on your structure, then you'd utilized this:

```
$my_user_name = $_get['user_name'];
```

So you start with a dollar sign ($) and an underscore character (_). Next comes the METHOD you need to utilize, POST or GET. You have to sort a couple of square sections next. In the middle of the square sections, you write the NAME of your HTML structure component – username, for our situation.

```
$_post['user_name'];
```

Obviously, you require the semi-colon to finish the line. Whatever the VALUE was for your HTML component is the thing that gets returned. You can then dole out this to a variable:

$my_user_name = $_post['user_name'];

So PHP will search for a HTML structure component with the NAME user_name. It then takes a gander at the VALUE characteristic for this structure component. It gives back this worth for you to utilize and control. Right now, everything we're doing is returning what the client entered and printing it to the page. Anyway, we can utilize a bit of Conditional Logic to test what is within the variable. As an illustration, change your PHP to this:

```
$my_user_name = $_post['user_name'];
if ($my_user_name == "letme") {
print ("Welcome User!");
}
else {
print ("You cannot access the website.");
}
```

We're currently verifying whether the client entered the content "letme". Provided that this is true, the user_-name is right; if not, print an alternate message. Attempt it out to see what happens. When you first load the page, before you even click the button, or else you may see the content " You cannot access the website." showed over the textbox. That is on account of the fact that we haven't verified whether the Submit on the structure was clicked.

Working Of Submit Button

In the last section, you perceived how to get content from a textbox when a Submit on a structure was clicked. Then again, when you first load the page, the content still shows. The motivation behind why the content showcases when the page is initially stacked is on account of the script executes whether the button is clicked or not.

This is the issue you confront when a PHP script is in agreement with the HTML, and is constantly submitted to itself in the ACTION property. To get around this, you can do a straightforward check, utilizing an alternate IF Statement. What you do is to check if the Submit was clicked. In the event that it was, go ahead and execute your code. To check if a submit was clicked, utilize the following piece of code:

```
if( isset( $_post['submit_1'] ) { }
```

You must think about the if proclamation. Anyhow in the middle of the round sections, we have isset( ). This is an inbuilt capacity that checks if a variable has been set or not. In the middle of the round sections, you write what you need to check using isset( ). For us, this is $_post['submit']. On the off chance that the client recently revived the page, then no worth will be set for the Submit. In the event that the client did click the Submit button, then PHP will consequently give back a value. Transform your script from the past page to the accompanying and attempt it out:

```
if (isset($_post['submit_1'])) {
$my_user_name = $_post['user_name'];
if ($my_user_name == "letme") {
print ("Welcome User!");
}
else {
print ("You cannot access the website.");
}
}
```

ACTION Attribute

You don't need to submit your structure information to the same PHP page, as we've been doing. You can send it to an altogether distinctive PHP page. To perceive how it functions, attempt this:

Make the accompanying page, and call it next_-

page_2.php. This is your HTML. Notice the ACTION attribute.

```
<html>
<head>
<title>Another HTML Form</title>
</head>
<body>
<form   name   ="form_1"   Method   ="post"   Action
="submit_form.php">
<input TYPE = "text" VALUE ="user_name" Name
="user_name">
<input TYPE = "Submit" Name = "Submit_1" VALUE
= "Login_value">
</Form>
</body>
</html>
```

Presently make the accompanying page, and call it submit_form.php:

```
<?php
$my_user_name = $_post['user_name'];
if ($my_user_name == "letme") {
print ("Welcome User!");
}
else {
print ("You cannot access this site.");
}
?>
```

In the PHP script above, notice how there are no HTML labels. Also we've forgotten the code that checks if Submit was clicked. That is on account of the fact that there is no PHP left in the first page. The code just gets executed IF the Submit is clicked.

Presenting structure information on an alternate PHP

script is an approach to keep the HTML and PHP separate. However there is an issue with it. The script gets executed on another page. That implies your structure will vanish!

Data Retention

As mentioned previously, at the point when the next_-page.php structure is submitted, the points of interest that the client entered get deleted. You're left with the VALUE that was situated in the HTML. For us, user_name continued showing up in the text box when the button was clicked. You can keep the information the client entered effortlessly. Your script ought to now resemble the one in the connection underneath. If not duplicate and glue this script, and test it out on your server.

On the off chance that you take a gander at the VALUE of the text box in the HTML from the above script, you'll see that it's set to "user_name". Since the structure gets presented again on itself, this worth will keep re-showing up in the textbox when the page is submitted. More regrettable, on the off chance that you've left the Value properties discharge, everything the client entered will vanish. This can be extremely irritating, in case you're asking the client to attempt once more.

A better approach is to POST back the values that the client entered. To post the subtle elements once again to the structure, and therefore keep the information the client has officially written out, you can utilize this:

Value="<?php print $user_name ; ?>"

As it were, the VALUE is currently a PHP line of code. The line of code is simply this:

```
<?php
print $user_name ;
?>
```

It's a bit hard to peruse, on the grounds that its all on one line.

You additionally need to change your PHP code in the HEAD segment to incorporate an else construct:

```
if (isset($_post['submit_1']))
{
$user_name = $_post['user_name'];
if($user_name == "letme") {
print ("Welcome User!");
}
else {
print ("You cannot access this site");
}
}
else {
$user_name ="";
}
```

In the else proclamation toward the end, we're simply setting the value of the variable called $user_name for when the button is NOT clicked, i.e. at the point when the page is revived. Be that as it may, there are some security issues connected with textboxes (and other structure components).

At the same time our new line of HTML for our textbox peruses like this:

```
<input TYPE = "text" Name ='user_name' Value="<?
php print $user_name ; ?>">
```

At the end of the day, we're presently printing out the VALUE with PHP code.

Radio Buttons

A Radio Button is an approach to limit clients to choose one of the options available. Cases are: Male/Female, Yes/No, or answers to studies and tests. To get the value of a radio button with PHP code, again you get to the NAME trait of the HTML structure components.

In the HTML page, the NAME of the Radio button is the same – "sex". The main Radio Button has an estimation of "male" and the second Radio Button has an estimation of female. When you're composing your PHP code, either of these values is returned. Here's some PHP code to illustrate this concept. You can add this code to the HEAD area of your HTML:

```
<?php
$selected_radio_button = $_post[sex];
print $selected_radio_button;
?>
```

This is pretty much the same code as we utilized for the content box! The main thing that is changed (other than the variable name) is the NAME of the HTML structure component we need to get to – "sex". The last line simply prints the value to the page. Once more, however, we can add code to discover if the client clicked Submit:

```
if (isset($_post['submit_1'])) {
$selected_radio_button = $_post['sex'];
print $selected_radio_button;
}
```

Once more, this is the same code you saw before. Simply, get to the structure component called "Submit_1" and check whether it is situated. The code just executes in the event that it is. Go for the code. Select a radio button and click Submit. The decision you made is printed to the page - either "male" or "female".

What you will perceive, in any case, when you go for the code is that the dab vanishes from your chosen radio button after Submit is clicked. Once more, PHP is not holding the value you chose. The answer for radio Buttons, however, is somewhat more mind boggling than for simple text boxes

Radio buttons have an alternate characteristic - checked or unchecked. You have to set which button was chosen by the client, so you need to compose PHP code inside the HTML with these qualities - checked or unchecked. Here's a way you can implement this:

```php
<?php
$male_button_status = 'unchecked';
$female_button_status = 'unchecked';
if (isset($_post['submit_1'])) {
$selected_radio_button = $_post['sex'];
if ($selected_radio_button = 'male') {
$male_button_status = 'checked';
}
else if ($selected_radio_button = 'female') {
$female_button_status = 'checked';
}
}
?>
```

Code for HTML Form

```html
<form name ="form_1" strategy ="post" activity ="radio_button_page.php">
<input sort = "Radio" Name = "sex" value= "male"
<?php print $male_button_status; ?>
>male
<input sort = "Radio" Name = "sex" value= "female"
<?php print $female_button_status; ?>
>female
<p>
<input sort = "Submit" Name = "Submit_1" VALUE = "Select one of the radio buttons.">
</Form>
```

Did we say somewhat more unpredictable? It is substantially more mind boggling than any code you've composed till now. Observe the PHP code inside the HTML first:

`<?php print $female_button_status; ?>`

This is simply a print statement. What is printed out is the value within the variable. What is within the variable will be either the saying "checked" or the statement "unchecked". Which of these it is relies on upon the rationale from our long PHP at the highest point of the page. How about we separate that.

Initially we have two variables at the highest point of the code:

`$male_button_status = 'unchecked';`

`$female_button_status = 'unchecked';`

These both get set to unchecked. That is just on the off chance that the page is refreshed, instead of the Submit being clicked.

Next we have our verify whether Submit is clicked:

`if (isset($_post['submit_1']){}`

This is done in precisely the same manner as done before. As is the following line that puts which radio catch was chosen into the variable:

`$selected_radio_button = $_post['sex'];`

We then need some conditional logic. We have to set a variable to "checked", so we have an if, else ... if development:

`if ($selected_radio_button == 'male') {`

`}`

`else if ($selected_radio_button == 'female') {`

`}`

Whatever we're doing is using what is within the variable called $selected_radio_button. In the event that its "male", you can do one thing. On the other hand, if its 'female', do an alternate thing. The code shown below illustrates how.

```
if ($selected_radio_button == 'male') {
$male_button_status = 'checked';
}
else if ($selected_radio_button = 'female') {
$female_button_status = 'checked';
}
```

On the off chance that the "male" radio button was clicked, the $male_button_status variable should be set to 'checked'. In the event that the "female" alternative was clicked, the $female_button_status variable should be set to 'checked'.

Working with Checkboxes

Like radio buttons, checkboxes are utilized to give guests options of alternatives to choose from. Though radio buttons confine clients to choose one of the presented options, you can choose more than one choice with checkboxes.

You don't need the ticks vanishing from the checkboxes, if the client has neglected to enter some different points of interest mistakenly. We saw with Radio Buttons that this can include some dubious coding. The same is valid for checkboxes.

When we coded for the Radio buttons, we gave the buttons the same NAME. That is on account of the fact that only a single alternative can be chosen with radio buttons. Since the client can choose more than one alternative with checkboxes, it bodes well to provide for them distinctive NAME values, and treat them as discrete elements.

In your PHP code, the procedure is to check whether every checkbox component has been checked or not. It's pretty much the same concerning the radio buttons. In the first place we set up five variable and set every one of them the unchecked, much the same as we did previously for radio buttons:

```
$check_box_1 = 'unchecked';
$check_box_2 = 'unchecked';
$check_box_3 = 'unchecked';
$check_box_4 = 'unchecked';
$check_box_5 = 'unchecked';
```

The following code checks if the submit button was clicked.

```
if (isset($_post['submit_1'])) {
}
```

Within this code, on the other hand, we have an alternate isset( ) capacity:

```
if ( isset($_post['cb_1']) ) {
}
```

This time, we're verifying whether a checkbox was clicked. We have to do this on account of an eccentricity of HTML checkboxes. On the off chance that they are not ticked, they have no value whatsoever, so nothing is returned! On the off chance that you attempt the code without checking if the checkboxes are ticked, then you'll need to manage a ton of "unclear" blunders.

On the off chance that the checkbox is ticked, however, it will give back a value. Thus, the isset( ) capacity will be true and the if code will be executed.

```
if($cb_1 == 'val_1') {
$cb_1 = 'checked';
}
```

This is yet an alternate If statement! Anyhow, we're simply checking the estimation of a variable. We have to comprehend what is within it. This one says, "If the quality within the variable called $cb_1 is "value_1" then execute some code. The code we have to execute is to put the content "checked" within the variable called $cb_1. Whatever remains of the if articulations are the same – one for every checkbox on the structure. The exact opposite thing we have to do is to print the value of the variable to the HTML structure:

```
<input sort = "checkbox" Name ='cb_1' value ="value_1"
<?php print $cb_1; ?>
>visual Basic .NET
```

Once more, this is the same code you saw with the radio buttons. The PHP part is:

```
<?php print $cb_1; ?>
```

So we're simply printing what is within the variable called $cb_1. This will either be "checked" or "unchecked." There are other answer for checkboxes, yet none appear basic! The point here, however, is that to take care of the concepts you learnt in the chapter on conditional logic.

LOOPS IN PHP

So what's a loop then? A loop is something that goes all around. In computer programs, it's precisely the same. But a programming loop will go all around until you let it know where to stop. You additionally need to tell the system two different things - where to begin your circle, and what to do after it's done one lap, which is also known as the upgrade declaration. You can program without utilizing loops. Anyway, using them makes your code compact and much simpler to comprehend.

In order to understand the concept of loops, consider the following example:

Consider a code where you need all numbers from 1 to 5. The answer to this coding problem is simply this:

$answer_val = 1 + 2 + 3 + 4 + 5;

print $answer_val;

Genuinely basic, you think. Also very little code, either. However consider the possibility that you needed to include a thousand numbers. Is it accurate to say that you are truly going to sort every one of them out like that? It's a horrendous parcel of writing. A loop would make life a ton less complex. You utilize them when you need to execute the same code again and again.

We'll examine a couple of kinds of programming loop in this chapter. However, the For Loop is the most utilized kind of loop, and this is why we will discuss the for loop first.

For Loops

For loop is the most commonly used looping construct in PHP. It is usually preferred over its counterparts because of its easy implementation and hassle-free comprehension. Here's a PHP For Loop in a little script. Add it into a new PHP script and save your work. Then run your code and test it out.

```php
<?php
$start_val = 1;
$count_val = 1;
for($start_val; $start_val <= 10; $start_val++) {
print $count_val . "<br>";
$count_val = $count_val + 1;
}
?>
```

How could you have been able to you get on? You ought to have seen the numbers 1 to 10 printed on your program page.

The general syntax for a for loop is:

for (starting value; ending value; update value expression) {
}

The principal thing you have to do is sort the name of the loop you're utilizing, which for this situation is for loop. In the middle of round brackets, you then place your three conditions:

Begin Value

The principal condition is the place you tell PHP the introductory value of your loop variable. In order, what should PHP start the loop with? We utilized this:

$start_val = 1;

We're allocating an estimation of 1 to a variable called $start_val. Like all variables, you can make up your name of the variable. A prominent name for the introductory variable is the letter i or j. You can set the starting condition before the loop starts, as we did:

$start_val = 1;

for($start_val; $start_val <= 10; $start_val++) {

On the other hand you can relegate your loop variable value right in the 'For Loop' code, as shown below:

for($start_val = 1; $start_val <= 10; $start_val++) {

The result is the same as the beginning number for this loop is 1.

End Value

Next, you need to advise PHP when to end your loop. This can be a number, a string, a Boolean value and any other expression or condition. Here, we're advising PHP to continue going round the loop while the estimation of the variable $start_val is lesser than or equal to 10.

for($start_val = 1; $start_val <= 10; $start_val++) {

At the point when the estimation of $start is 11, PHP will end the loop and come out of the scoping brace.

Upgrade Expression

Loops require a method for getting the next number for looping variable, which is given in the form of an update expression in the for structure. On the off chance that the loop couldn't upgrade the beginning value, it would be stuck on the beginning value. As it were, you have to advise the circle how it is to go all around. We utilized this:

$start_val++

In a ton of programming languages (and PHP), the twofold or more operators (++) implies addition (expand the quality by one). It's simply a short method for saying this:

$start_val = $start_val + 1

You can decrement the value in the same manner by utilizing the twofold less operator (- -), yet we won't go into that.

So our entire loop peruses "Beginning at an estimation of 1, continue going all around while the value of the looping variable is short of 11 and update the beginning value by one each time the loop is executed."

Each time the loop goes round, the code between our two wavy sections { } gets executed:

print $count_val . "<br>";

$counter = $count_val + 1;

Perceive that we're simply augmenting the counter variable by 1 each one time round the circle, precisely in the same way as we are doing with the start_val variable. So we could have put this:

$count_val ++

The impact would be the same. As a trial, have a go at setting the estimation of $count_val to 11 outside the circle, which is at present $count_val = 0. At that point inside the circle, use $counter- - (the twofold less sign). Could you think about what will happen? Will it crash, or not? On the other hand will it print something out? Better save your work, in the event that something goes wrong!

While Loop

As opposed to utilizing a for circle, you have the choice to utilize a while loop. The structure of a while loop is more basic than a for loop, on the grounds that you're just assessing one condition. The loop goes all around while the condition is true. At the point when the condition is false, it breaks out of the whole circle. Here's the syntax:

```
while (testing_condition) {
//Code
}
```

The following code illustrates the implementation of a while loop.

```
$count_val = 1;
while ($count_val < 11) {
print ("count_val = " . $count_val . "<br>");
$count_val++;
}
```

The condition to test for is $count_val < 11. Each one time round the whole circle, that condition is checked. In the event that count_val is short of eleven, then the condition is true. At the point when $counter is more noteworthy than eleven then the condition is false. A while circle will quit going all around when a condition is false.

In the event that you utilize a while circle, be cautious that you don't make an infinite loop. You'd make one of these on the off chance that condition yields a true in all cases.

Do-While Loop

This sort is loop is very nearly indistinguishable to the whole circle, aside from the fact that the condition has a go at toward the end:

```
do
{
//Code
}while (testing_condition)
```

The distinction is that your code gets executed in any event at least once. In an ordinary while circle, the condition could be met before your code gets executed and the loop will be exited right away. However, here the condition is checked after the loop code has executed once.

Don't stress excessively over do ... while loops. Focus on for loops for practical programming purposes. At the same time, there is an alternate kind of loop that proves to be useful, which is also called the For Each loop. However, it is rarely used and thus we have chosen to skip its description altogether.

Break Keyword

There are times when you have to break out of a loop before the entire thing gets executed. Alternately, you need to break unaware of what's going on in light of a lapse that your code or client may have made. In such a case, you can utilize the break keyword. Luckily, this includes just writing break followed by a semicolon.

16

ARRAYS

By now, it is imperative that you comprehend what a variable is – simply a stockpiling territory where you hold numbers and text. The issue is, a variable will hold one and only one value at a time. You can store a solitary number in a variable, or a solitary string. An array is similar to any unique variable, which can hold more than one number, or more than one string, at once. On the off chance that you have a list of things (like client requests, for instance), and you have to do something with them, then it would be very awkward to do this:

    $order_1 = "Shoes Variety 1";
    $order_2 = "Shoes Variety 2";
    $order_3 = "Shoes Variety 3";
    $order_4 = "Shoes Variety 4";

You may use a loop through your requests and discover a particular one or access records and make changes to them one by one. What's more, imagine a scenario where you had not four requests, but you have more than four hundred of these. A solitary variable is plainly not the best programming apparatus to use here. In this case, an array is one of the more practically feasible storage options for you. An array can hold all your requests under a solitary name. Furthermore you can get to the requests by simply alluding to the array name followed by the index of the concerned request.

In order to set up an array, you can use the following syntax:

$order_array = array( );

To start with you write out what you need your cluster to be called ($order_array, in the example shown above) and, after an equivalents sign, you write this:

array( );

So, setting up an array simply includes writing the expression array, followed by a couple of round brackets. This is sufficient to advise PHP that you need to set up the array. Be that as it may, there's nothing in the cluster yet. Whatever we're doing with our line of code is advising PHP to set up an array, and provide for it the name $order_array.

Adding Elements To The Array

You can utilize two essential strategies to place something into an array.

Strategy One – Type between the round sections

The primary strategy includes writing your values between the round sections of array(). In the code beneath, we're setting up a cluster to hold the types of coats in your wardrobe:

$coat_types = array("Winter Coats", "Summer Coats", "Short Coats", "Over Coats");

So the name of the array is $coat_types. Between the round sections of array(), we have written a few values. Each one value is differentiated by a comma.

Arrays work by having a position, and some information

for that position. In the above array, "Winter Coast" is in position zero, "Summer Coats" is in position 1, "Short Coats" is in position 2, and "Over Coats" is in position 3.

The main position is constantly zero, unless you tell PHP otherwise. Anyhow the position is know as a key. The key then has a worth connected to it. You can detail your own particular numbers for the keys in the following manner:

$coat_types = array(1 => "Winter Coats", 2 => "Summer Coats", 3 => "Short Coats", 4 => "Over Coats");

So, you write a number for your key, emulated by the equivalents sign and a right plot section (=>). In the exhibit over, the first Key is currently 1 and not 0. The thing put away under key 1 is "Winter Coats". The last key is 4, and the thing put away under key 4 is "Over Coats". Watchful of every one of the commas, when you set up an array like this.

Technique two – Assign values to a cluster

An alternate approach to place values into an array in a manner similar to this:

$coat_types = show();
$coat_types[ ]="Winter Coats";
$coat_types[ ]="Summer Coats";
$coat_types[ ]="Short Coats";
$coat_types[ ]="Over Coats";

Here, the array is initially created with $coat_types = array();. This advises PHP that you need to make an array with the name of $coat_types. To store values in the exhibit you first sort the name of the cluster, emulated by a couple of square sections:

$coat_types[ ]

After the equivalents sign, you write out what you need to store in this position. Since no numbers were written in the middle of the square sections, PHP will allot the number o as the first key:

o=> "Winter Coats",

1=> "Summer Coats",

2=> "Short Coats",

3=> "Over Coats"

Accessing Array Elements

Actually, there are few ways you can do it. Yet the "Key" is the key. Here's an illustration for you to attempt:

```
<?php
$coat_types = array("Winter Coats", "Summer Coats", "Short Coats", "Over Coats");
print $coat_types[o];
?>
```

The array is the same one we set up some time recently. To get at what is within a cluster, simply sort the key number you need to get to. In the above code, we're printing out what is held in the o position (Key) in the array. You must simply place the key number between the square sections of your show name in the following manner:

print $array_name[o];

Associative Arrays

Your clusters keys don't need to be numbers, as in the past segment. They can be strings as well. This can help you recollect what's in a key, or what it should do. When you utilize content for the keys, you're utilizing an associative cluster; when you utilize numbers for the keys, you're utilizing a scalar array. Here's a cluster that sets up first name and surname consolidations:

```
$name = array( );
$name["nick"] = "Carter";
$name["richard"] = "Waters";
```

To get to the values in an associative array, simply allude to the Key name:

print $name["nick"];

Notwithstanding, on the grounds that associative arrays don't have numbers for the keys, an alternate system is utilized to loop around them – the For Each loop.

Sorting Arrays

There may be times when you need to sort the values within an array. Case in point, assume your array elements are not in order. Like this one:

$name = array( );
$name["nick"] = "Carter";
$name["richard"] = "Waters";

To sort this array, you simply utilize the asort( ) function. This includes nothing more intricate than writing the statement asort, emulated by round sections. In the middle of the round sections, sort for the sake of your associative:

asort($name);

Different functions that can be utilized to sort values in shows include:

rsort( ) – Sorts a scalar array in converse request

arsort( ) - Sorts the values of an associative cluster in opposite request

krsort( ) - Sorts the keys of an associative cluster in opposite request

Getting Random Keys

You can get a random key from a cluster. This could be valuable in some coding scenarios.

```
<?php
$number_array = array(1 => 1, 2 => 2, 3 => 3, 4 => 4, 5 => 5, 6 => 6);
$random_key_element = array_rand($number_array, 1);
print $random_key_element;
```

?>

The function that furnishes a proportional key is this:

array_rand($number_array, 1);

You begin off with the function array_rand( ). In the middle of the round sections, you require two things: the name of your array, and what number of keys you need.

The Count Function in PHP

The count( ) function is valuable when you need to return what number of components are there in your array.

To get what number of components are in the cluster, we utilized this:

$array_count = count($coat_types);

STRING MANIPULATION

The function take strings of content and control them is one of the key capacities you require as a developer. In the event that a client enters subtle elements on your structures, then you have to check and accept this information. Generally, this will include doing things to this text.

Some examples of these manipulations include changing over letters from lowercase to uppercase or vis-a-versa, checking which program the client has or cutting down on white space from content entered in a content box. These go under the heading of string control. To make a beginning, we'll take a gander at changing the case of character.

Changing the Case of a Character

Assume a you have a textbox on a structure that asks clients to enter a first name and surname. The chances are high that somebody will enter this:

jack waters

Rather than this:

Jack Waters

So your work as a developer is to change over the first

letter of each one name to uppercase from lower. This is simple, with PHP. It's simply a textbox and a button. The textbox will have "jack waters" entered, when you stack it up. What we need to do is to transform it to "Jack Waters" when the button is clicked. Here's the script that does that.

```php
<?php
$name = 'jack waters';
if(isset($_post['submit_1'])) {
$name = $_post['user_name'];
$name = ucwords( $name );
}
?>
```

The primary line simply verifies that the lowercase adaptation is put into the textbox when the page loads:

$name = 'jack waters';

This is the line that we need to change over and turn into" "Jack Waters". The main line in the code that you haven't yet met is this one:

$name = ucwords($name);

What's more, that is everything you need to change over the first letter of each saying to uppercase. The inbuilt function that is used for this purpose is:

ucwords( )

In the middle of the round sections, you need to write the variable or content you need to change over. PHP will deal with the rest. At the point when the change is finished, we're putting it away into the variable called $name.

In the event that you simply need to change over the first letter of a string (for a sentence, for instance), then you can use ucfirst( ) .

Trimming White Space

Something else you'll need to do is to trim the white (clear) space from content entered into textboxes. This is simple, as there's some helpful PHP inbuilt-functions to help you do this. Assume your client has entered this in the textbox:

" user_name "

From the quotes, we can see that there is additional space in the text, before and after the main content. We can count what number of characters this string has with an alternate valuable capacity: strlen( ). As its name proposes, this gives back where its due of a string. By length, we mean what number of characters a string has. Attempt this script:

```
<?php
$w_space = " user_name ";
$count_val = strlen($w_space);
print $count_val;
?>
```

When you run the script, you'll find that the variable contains 15 characters. Notwithstanding, user_name has just 9 characters. In case you're checking for a precise match, this matters!

To uproot the white space, you can utilize the trim( ) capacity. Change your script to this:

```
<?php
$w_space = trim(" user_name ");
$count_val = strlen($w_space);
print $count_val;
?>
```

When you run the script now, you ought to find that the variable has the right number of characters - 9. That is on account of the trim( ) capacity expels any clear spaces from the left and right of a string. Two related functions are ltrim( ) and rtrim( ). The first, ltrim( ), expels space from the earliest starting point of a string; the second one, rtrim( ), expels space from the end of a string.

The strpos Function

A more helpful thing you'll need to do is to check whether one string is within an alternate. Case in point, you can get which program the client has with this:

$client = $_server["http_user_client"];

print $client;

Attempt it out and see what gets printed out. You ought to find that this string gets printed. In case you're trying which program the client has, you can utilize a string function to look for a short string within this long one. A PHP string function you can utilize is strpos( ). The sentence structure for the strpos function is:

strpos(string_to_consider, string_to_find, begin)

Part Lines

To part lines of content, the explode ( ) function can be utilized. You recently gave it the content you need to part, and the character that is utilized to discrete each one piece. Here's the sentence structure:

explode(separator, string_to_split)

In the middle of the round sections of explode( ), the separator you need to utilize goes initially, emulated by a comma, then the string you need to part. For our line of code above, you'd do this:

$line_text = "Numbers 1, 450, 3500, 264, 500, 7869";

$line_text = explode("," , $line_text);

So basically we're stating, "search for a comma in the content, and part the line of content into particular pieces." Once PHP does its employment, it puts all the parts into the variable on the left hand side of the equivalents sign (=), which was $line_text for us. This variable will then be an array!

Joining Strings

In the event that you have a line of content in a array,

you can go along with everything together to structure a solitary line of content. This is the polar opposite of explode. This time, make use of implode( ):

$coat_type = array("Winter Coats", "Summer Coats", "Short Coats", "Over Coats");

$line_new = implode(",", $coat_type);

Here, we have an array called $coat_type. The content in the array needs to be joined before keeping in touch with it again to a content record. The implode( ) function does the joining. The structure for the implode( ) function is similar to that of explode( ).

implode(separator, texts_to_join)

So, implode( ) will join all the content together and separate each one section with a comma, in the code above. Obviously, you don't need to utilize a comma as a rule. You could utilize whatever other character.

Escape Characters in PHP

Escape sequence in PHP doesn't mean breaking free and "doing a runner". It is a method to keep PHP from terminating your strings too soon, or for verifying you have the right string data returned. Here's an illustration. Attempt this script:

```
<?php
$my_string = 'This is Sarah's car';
print $my_string;
?>
```

Verify you write the script precisely as it is, with all the single quote imprints. Next, run the script. What you ought to discover is that PHP provides for you a message of error. The reason is that you have three single quote imprints. PHP gets confounded, in light of the fact that it doesn't realize what your string is. To tackle the issue, you could utilize twofold quotes on the outside. Like this:

$my_string = "This is Sarah's car";

Then again you could get away from the punctuation. You get away from a character by writing a "\" before it. Like this:

$my_string = 'This is Sarah\'s car';

On the off chance that you attempt that out, you ought to find that the string prints perfectly.

Now attempt this script:

```
<?php
$new_string = 'mypath\';
print $new_string;
?>
```

Once more, you'll get a message from PHP citing an error in your code. Encompass it with twofold quotes rather than single quotes and run the script once more. Does the string print? The reason it doesn't is on account of you haven't gotten away from the escape character. PHP sees it as an uncommon character, and is expecting more subtle elements after the back-slash. In order to avoid such a lapse, you can use the following code:

$new_string = 'mypath\\';

So now we have two cuts on the end of the string. When you run the script, you ought to observe that it prints out this:

mypath\

In the event that your PHP script is not giving back it's due that it is ought to do, then you may need to utilize the slice to escape them. You additionally need to escape certain characters when working with databases, else, you're opening yourself up to a long list of error messages and warnings.

Some Important String Functions

As opposed to enumerating all the conceivable string

functions you can utilize, we'll simply provide for you a concise list. There's a case of how to utilize each one string function, in the event that you click on the connections beneath. Simply make use of them as and when required.

ord( ): determines a character's ASCII value

chr( ): performs conversion of ASCII value to character

similar_text( ): determines the similarity between two text strings

echo( ): used as an alternative to print

substr( ): returns a substring from the string

str_replace( ): performs replacement of one string from another

str_repeat( ): performs repetition of characters a specified number of times

strlen( ): returns the string length

str_word_count( ): returns the number of words in a string

FUNCTIONS IN PHP

A function is simply a section of code. However, it is different from your main code. You separate it on the grounds that its decent and helpful, and you need to utilize it not once but again and again. It's a piece of code that you think is valuable, and need to utilize once more. Functions spare you from composing the code again and again.

Assume you have to check content from a textbox. You need to trim any clear spaces from the left and right of the content that the client entered. So on the off chance that they entered this:

" Jack Waters "

You need to transform it into this:

"Jack Waters"

In any case you additionally need to check if the client entered any content whatsoever. You don't need the textbox to be totally clear. You can utilize the PHP inbuilt capacity called trim( ) for solving this purpose.

$entered_text = trim($_post['text_1']);

That will dispose off the white space in the text box.

Anyhow it won't check if the content box is clear. You can include an if articulation for that:

```
if ($entered_text == "") {
error_message = "Nothing written in the text box";
}
```

Yet suppose it is possible that you have loads of textboxes on your structure. You'd need to have heaps of if proclamations, and check each one single variable for a clear string. That is a ton of code to compose! Instead of doing that, you can make a solitary function, with one if articulation that can be utilized for each one clear string you have to check.

Utilizing a function means there's less code for you to compose. What's more, its more effective. We'll perceive how to compose a function for the above situation in a minute. Anyhow first and foremost, here's the syntax structure for a function.

```
function function_name() {
}
```

So you begin by writing the statement function. You then need to think of a name for your function. You can call it very nearly anything you like. It's much the same as a variable_name. Next, you write two round sections ( ). At long last, you require the two wavy sections also { }. Whatever you do goes between the wavy sections. Here's a straightforward sample that simply print something out:

```
function print_message() {
print "Error!";
}
```

In the case above, we've begun with the word function. We've then called this specific function print_message().In the middle of the wavy sections, there a print articulation. Attempt it out with this script:

```php
<?php
function print_message() {
print "Error!";
}
?>
```

Run your script and see what happens. You ought to find that nothing happens! The reason that nothing happened is on account of a capacity is a different bit of code. It doesn't run until you let it know to. Simply stacking the script won't work. It's similar to those inbuilt capacities you utilized, for example, trim.

You can't utilize trim( ) unless you write out the name, and what you need PHP to trim. The same applies to your own particular functions – you need to "tell" PHP that you need to utilize a function that you composed. You do this by just writing out the name of your function. This is known as "calling" a function. Attempt this new form of the script.

```php
<?php
function print_message() {
print "Error!";
}
print_message();
?>
```

After the capacity, we've written out the name once more. This is sufficient to advise PHP to run our code portion. Presently, change your code to this, and see what happens:

```php
<?php
print_message();
function print_message() {
print "Error!";
}
?>
```

On the off chance that you have PHP 4 or above, you ought to see no distinction – the function will in any case get executed with the name above or underneath the function. Yet for tidiness and coherence's purpose, it's better to put the greater part of your function either at the top or base of your scripts. Then again exceeding all expectations even further, in a different PHP document. You can then utilize an alternate inbuilt function called "include."

Function Scope

There's a thing called scope in programming. This alludes to where in your scripts a variable can be seen. In the event that a variable can be seen from anyplace, it's said to have global scope of functioning. In PHP, variables within capacities can't be seen from outside of the capacity. What's more, functions can't see variables in the event that they are not piece of the capacity itself. Attempt this variety of our script as a case:

```php
<?php
$err_message = "Error Found!";
print_message();
function print_message( ) {
print $err_message;
}
?>
```

This time, we have set up a variable called $err_message to hold the content of our message. This is situated up outside of the function. Run the script, and you'll get a PHP error message about " Undefined variable".

In like manner, attempt this script:

```php
<?php
print_message();
print $err_text;
function print_message() {
```

```php
$err_text = "Error!";
}
?>
```

This time, the variable is inside the function. However, we're attempting to print it from outside the function. Regardless, you get a blunder message. Here's a right form:

```php
<?php
print_message();
function print_message() {
$err_text = "Error!";
print $err_text;
}
?>
```

Here, we have both the variable and the print explanation set up within the capacity. The mistake message now prints.

So on the off chance that you have to inspect what is within a variable, you require an approach to get the variable to the capacity. That is the place contentions come in.

Arguments

Functions can be given variables, with the goal that you can do something with what's within them. You ignore the variable to your function by writing them within the round sections of the function name. Here's a script like the one you saw prior:

```php
<?php
$err_text = "Error!";
print _message($err_text);
function print_message($err_text) {
print $err_text;
}
?>
```

The main contrast is the that we now have something between the round sections of our function:

function print_message($err_text) {
}

The name is the same, yet we've put a variable in the middle of the round sections. This is the variable that we need to do something with. The one called $err_text. By writing a variable within the round sections, you are setting up something many refer to as an argument. An argument is a variable or value that you need your capacity to manage.

Calling Functions

$err_text = "Error!";
print_message($err_text);

The first line places something into the variable. Anyhow, when you need to hand something to a function that has an argument, you have to write it in the function call. In our script, we're writing the name of the variable.

However, if you attempt to call this function without giving any argument, like shown below, you can expect to get an error message from PHP.

print_message( );

That is letting you know that your function has been set up to take an argument, yet that you've left the round sections void when you attempted to call the function. Your functions can have more than 1 arguments. Simply separate every argument with a comma. A sample implementation of this sort is given below:

function check_for_errors($err_text, err_flag) {
}

Getting Values From Functions

When you're making your function, you may recognize that they can be softened down up to two classes: functions that you can leave, and simply let them do their tasks; and functions where you have to recover an answer. As a sample, here's the two separate classes in activity:

```
print ("Message!");
$str_len = strlen($str_len);
```

The print function is a sample of a function that you can leave, and simply let it do its tasks. You simply let it know what to print and it gets on with it for you. On the other hand, a function like strlen( ) is definitely not. You need something back from it – the length of the string.

Assume you had a function that worked out a 20 percent markdown. Anyhow, you just need to apply the markdown if the client used in excess of 100 pounds. You could make a function that is given the sum used. At that point verify whether its over a 100 pounds. In the event that it is, the function ascertains the rebate; if not, don't worry about the markdown. In both cases, you need the function to give back where its due to your inquiry – What do I charge this client? Here's the script:

```
<?php
$t_expenditure = 200;
$total_order = compute_order_total($t_expenditure);
print $total_order;
function compute_order_total($t_expenditure) {
$discount = 0.2;
if ($t_expenditure > 100) {
$t_discount = $t_expenditure - ($t_expenditure *
$discount);
$t_charge = $t_discount;
}
else {
$t_charge = $t_expenditure;
}
return $t_charge;
```

```
}
?>
```

The lines to focus on are the ones for the $t_expenditure variable. The code first sets up an aggregate sum used, which in practice may originate from a structure on a content box, or a shrouded field:

```
$t_expenditure = 200;
```

The following line is our function call:

```
$total_order = compute_order_total($t_expenditure);
```

The function call is currently on the right of the equivalents sign (=). To the left of the equivalents sign is simply an ordinary variable - $total_order. In case you're setting up your function like this, then you are asking PHP to give back a value from your functions, and put the answer into a variable on the left of the equivalents sign.

PHP will go off and figure your function. When it discovers an answer, it will attempt to give back a value. The answer will be put away for the sake of your function, compute_order_total( ) for us. Anyhow take a gander at the function itself, and the line toward the end:

```
function compute_order_total($t_expenditure) {
$discount = 0.2;
if($t_expenditure > 100) {
$t_discount = $t_expenditure - ($t_expenditure * $discount);
$t_charge = $t_discount;
}
else {
$t_charge = $t_expenditure;
}
return $t_charge;
}
```

The last line is:

return $t_charge;

The return word advises PHP to give back a value. The value it returns is whatever you have put away in the variable that comes after the statement return. Here, were advising PHP to situated the response to the function called compute_order_total( ) to whatever is put away in the variable we've called $t_charge. It's this that will get put away in our variable called $total_order.

In case you are discovering this a bit precariously, recall what a function is: a different bit of code that does some work for you. It can either give back a value, or not give back a value. It depends completely on your needs.

Calling a Function by Reference or Value

Functions can be difficult to use, in the event that you've never utilized them previously. An alternate troublesome part to comprehend is the manner by which values can change, or not change, contingent upon extension. Scope, on the off chance that you review, alludes to where in your code a variable can be seen. On the off chance that you simply do this, for instance:

```
$var_val = 50;
case( );
function case() {
print $var_val;
}
```

In place for the function to have the capacity to see what's within the variable called $var_val, you can set up the function to acknowledge an argument. You'd then sort the variable name between the round sections, when you call it. This has been illustrated in the following code:

```
<?php
$var_val = 25;
ex_func($var_val);
```

```
function ex_func($var_val) {
print $var_val;
}
?>
```

In the event that you run the code above, it now prints out the number twenty five. At the same time, it is critical to understand that you are simply giving the function a duplicate of the variable. Any changes made to the code shall not affect the variable in the code of the calling function. As a case, change your code to this:

```
<?php
$var_val = 25;
print "Before the function call = " . $var_val . "<br>";
ex_func($var_val);
print "After the function call = " . $var_val;
function ex_func($var_val) {
$var_val = $var_val + 25;
print "Within the function = " . $var_val . "<br>";
}
?>
```

Here, we have three print structures: one preceding the call to the function, one within the function, and one after the function call. Yet we're printing out the estimation of the variable called $var_val each one time. Within the function, we're adding 25 to the estimation of the variable. When you run the code, it will print out this:

Prior to the function call = 25
Within the function = 50
After the function call = 25

The critical one is after the function call. Despite the fact that we changed the estimation of $var_val within the function, regardless it print 25 after the function call! That is on account of the capacity was given a duplicate, and NOT the first.

When you hand a function a duplicate of a variable, it is called passing the variable by value (simply a duplicate). The option is to NOT pass a duplicate, however to allude once more to the first. Roll out one little improvement to your script. This is the sample code for this scenario.

function ex_func(&$var_val) {

The main expansion is a & character before the variable between round sections. This advises PHP that you need to roll out improvements to the first, and don't simply need a duplicate. When you run the script, it now print out the accompanying:

Prior to the capacity call = 10

Within the capacity = 20

After the capacity call = 20

After the capacity call, we now have an estimation of 20! So a change to the estimation of the variable outside the capacity has been made. When you rolls out improvements to the first like this current, its called passing the variable by reference

Server Variables in PHP

PHP stores data about the server. This will entail things like, the program the guest is utilizing, the IP location, and which site page the guest originated from. Here's a script to attempt with those three server variables:

$browsing_program = $_server['http_user_agent'];

$referring_agent = $_server['http_referring_agent'];

$ip_address = $_server['remote_address'];

print "IP Adress = " . $ipaddress;

print "Program = " . $browser . "<br>";

print "Referrer = " . $referrer . "<br>";

These are valuable in the event that you need to log

your details, or to boycott a specific IP address. On the off chance that you run the script on a neighbourhood machine, you may get an error message for the referrer.

So to get at the qualities in server variables, the sentence structure is this:

$_server['server_variable']

You begin with a dollar sign, then an underscore character ($_). At that point you include the expression SERVER. In the middle of square sections, you write the name of the server variable you need to get to. Encompass this with either single or twofold quotes.

Since you are giving back a value, you have to put all that on the right hand side of an equivalents sign. On the left of the equivalents sign (=), you require a variable to hold the string that is returned. The server variables are held in an array, so you can utilize a foreach circle to get a list of all accessible ones.

Header Function

When you ask for a site page to be brought once more to your program, you're not simply bringing back the page. You're likewise bringing back something many refer to as a HTTP HEADER. This is some additional data, for example, kind of system making the appeal, date asked for, if it be shown as a HTML report, to what extent the archive is, and much more.

One of the things HTTP HEADER likewise does is to give status data. This could be whether the page was discovered (404 errors), and the area of the archive. In the event that you need to redirect your clients to an alternate page, here's a sample:

```
<?php
header("location: http://www.homeandlearn.co.uk/");
?>
```

```
<html>
<body>
</body>
</html>
```

Note how the header code goes before any HTML. In the event that you put header code after the HTML, you'll get an error message along the lines of "header data cannot be changed."

Include Function

Having the capacity to incorporate different documents into your HTML code, or for your PHP scripts, is a valuable thing. The include( ) function permits you to do this. Assume you have a document that you need to incorporate in an online page. You could duplicate and glue the content from the record straight into you HTML. On the other hand, you can also utilize the include( ) function for the same purpose.

WORKING WITH FILES

The capacity to open up records, for example, plain text or CSV documents is an extraordinary resource for you as a developer. Not every task obliges a database with various tables, and put away straightforward information in a record can be a decent option. This is true particularly if your web host doesn't permit you to have a database.

Opening A File

To open up a record, there are a couple of techniques you can utilize. The one we'll begin with is readfile( ). As its name propose, it peruses the content of a file or record for you. Attempt this basic script for an introduction to file handling in PHP.

```
<?php
$doc_value = readfile( "my_dictionary.txt" );
print $doc_value;
?>
```

The readfile( ) function is valuable if all you need to do is open up a record and read its content.

An alternate function that simply peruses the substance

of a record is file_get_contents( ). It is accessible in PHP rendition 4.3 or more. Here's a case:

```php
<?php
$file_for_reading = "my_dictionary.txt";
print file_get_contents( $file_for_reading );
?>
```

This is utilized as a part of pretty much the same path as the readfile function. The distinction for us is the change of name to file_get_contents( ). A finer strategy to open records is with fopen( ). This function provides for you more alternatives that, for example, setting whether the record is for perusing, for keeping in touch with too, and a couple of more choices. Here's a case:

```php
<?php
$doc_value = fopen( "my_dictionary.txt", "r" );
print $doc_value;
fclose($doc_value);
?>
```

Run this script and see what happens. You ought to see something like the accompanying printed out:

Resource ID #2

Not exactly what you were anticipating! The reason is that fopen( ) doesn't really perused the content of a record. Everything it does is to situate a pointer to the record you need to open. It then returns what's called a document handle. Whatever you're doing is advising PHP to recollect the area of the record.

The "r" on the end signifies "open this petition for perusing only". We'll see different alternatives in a minute. Yet, now that you've advised PHP to recollect the area of the record you need to open, how would you read the content of the document?

One path is to utilize fgets( ). This will read an indicated number of character on a solitary line of content. It's regularly used for looping and reads each one line of content. When you're utilizing fgets( ), you likewise need to check when the end of the document has been arrived at. This is finished with the inbuilt capacity feof - record, end of document.

$file_handler = fopen("my_dictionary.txt", "r");

In addition, there are different alternatives. The value 'r' can be used for read-only, 'w' for write-only, 'r+' and 'w+' for read and write, 'a' for append and 'a+' for append and read.

Checking If The Record Exists

It's a decent thought to check if the record exists, before attempting to do something with it. The file_exists( ) function can be utilized for this:

if(file_exists("my_dictionary_2.txt") {

print "This file exists!";

}

else {

print "This file does not exist.";

}

To begin with, we ask PHP to open the record and make a document handle:

$file_handler = fopen("test_file.txt", "w");

So we're asking PHP to make a document handle that indicates a content record called "test_file.txt". In the event that a document of this name can't be discovered, then one will be made with this name. After a comma, we've written "w". This tells PHP that the document will be opened for writing only.

The third line is the place we manipulate the record:

fwrite($file_handler, $doc_value);

In the middle of the round sections of fwrite( ), we've set

two things: the document we need to keep in touch with, and the content of the record. Also, with the exception of shutting the document, that is everything you need!

file_put_contents( )

On the off chance that you have PHP 5, you can utilize the new function called file_put_contents( ) rather than fwrite( ).

It is used in the same manner as file_put_contents() with the only difference of a third parameter.

file_put_contents($file_handler, $doc_value, setting);

The setting choice can be File_append and File_use_include_path.

So to attach to the record, simply do this:

file_put_contents($file_handler, $doc_value, File_append);

Perusing a Text File And Saving It In An Array

There is an alternate choice you can use to place lines of content into a cluster. In the strategy beneath, we're utilizing the explode( ) string to make an array from each one line of content. Here's the code:

```php
<?php
$file_handler = fopen("my_dictionary.txt", "rb");
while (!feof($file_handler) ) {
$text_lines = fgets($file_handler);
$parts_of_line = explode('=', $text_lines);
print $parts_of_line[0] . $parts_of_line[1]. "<br>";
}
fclose($file_handler);
?>
```

Document Locations

There are a couple of inbuilt PHP functions you can use to discover document ways. This is helpful for discovering the careful area (relative or supreme) of your scripts or pages. Before you attempt these out, make another PHP page and save it as file_dir.php.

The following code can be used for determining the path of a file.

```
<?php
$absolutepath = realpath("file_dir.php");
print "Path: " . $absolutepath;
?>
```

To get the accurate way of document, then, you can utilize real_path(). In the middle of the round sections of the function, sort the name of the record. The following code is used to get the directory, yet not the document name.

```
<?php
$dir_name = dirname("folder/myphp/file_dir.php");
print "Index is: " . $dir . "<br>";
?>
```

In order to get the names of the directory, you can utilize the function dirname( ). This will strip off the name of the record and furnish a proportional payback of the content between the round sections of the capacity.

However, if you wish to get the name of the file, you can use te following code:

```
<?php
$base_name = basename("folder/myphp/file_dir.php");
print "Name of the document is: " . $base_name . "<br>";
?>
```

If you have to get the name of the document, then utilize the function basename( ). When you write a more drawn out record way in the middle of the round sections of the capacity, it will strip off the rest and leave the name of the document.

TIME AND DATE FUNCTIONS IN PHP

Knowing how to handle time and date values in PHP will be a valuable expansion to your programming abilities. In this and the accompanying segments, we'll investigate how to process this sort of information.

The date( ) function

The inbuilt PHP function date( ) is the most generally utilized strategy for returning date values. Sadly, there is a long rundown of things you can put between the round sections of the capacity! Attempt this script, to get a thought of how it functions:

```
<?php
$day_today = date('d-m-y');
print $day_today;
?>
```

It ought to print the day of the week first (d), then the month (m), then the year (y). Be that as it may, this will be the numerical arrangement. So it will print something like:

21-10-2014

An alternate helpful date/time function is getdate( ). This will give back an associative array with all the time and date values. You can utilize it for things like contrasting one date with an alternate. For instance, looking at how long have passed since a given date. Here's the syntax for using this function:

getdate(time_stamp); The time stamp is non-compulsory. In the event that you forget it, it gets the values for the current neighbourhood time and date.

Since getdate gives back an associative array, you can simply do this kind of thing:

$day_today = getdate();

print $day_today['mday'];

print $day_today['wday'];

print $day_today['yday'];

So whichever piece of the array you need to get to goes between square sections. You then sort one of the keys between quote marks.

PHP AND MYSQL

PHP can associate with and control databases. The most prevalent database framework that is utilized with PHP is called Mysql. This is a free database framework, and accompanies the Wampserver programming you may have introduced toward the begin of the course. We will be working with Mysql databases all through these lessons.

Opening a Connection to a MySql Database

PHP has a considerable measure of inbuilt functions you can use to control databases. In PHP 5, a considerable measure more were included too! Here, we'll stay with the inbuilt functions for adaptations sooner than PHP 5. Anyhow, on the off chance that you have form 5, its well worth scrutinizing the fresher database capacities. A decent place to begin is php_page.net. To open our Customer Records database, we'll utilize the accompanying inbuilt capacities:

```
mysql_connect()
mysql_select_db()
mysql_close()
```

The approached we'll make has three strides. Here is an elaborated discussion on each of these steps.

Step 1 - Open an association with MySql

The main occupation is to connect with MySql. As its name recommends, mysql_connect( ) does precisely that.

Step 2 - Specify the database you need to open

In our code, we set up a variable with the name of our database:

$database_name = "customerrecords";

Step 3 - Close the association

Shutting an association with a database is simple. In the event that you've utilized a record handle, you simply do this:

mysql_close($db_handle);

Perusing Records

To peruse records from a database, the method is as a rule to loop and find the ones you need. To tag which records you need, you utilize something many refer to as SQL. This stands for Structured Query Language. This is a regular, non-coding dialect that uses words like SELECT and WHERE. At its least difficult level, it's genuinely direct. Be that as it may, the more unpredictable the database, the more trickier the SQL is. We'll begin with something basic however. What we need to do, now that we have an association with our database, is to peruse all the records, and print them out to the page.

Structured Query Language

SQL is an approach to question and control databases. The fundamentals are not difficult to learn. On the off chance that you need to snatch the majority of the records from a table in a database, you utilize the word, SELECT. This can be done in the following manner:

SELECT * FROM Name_of_table

SQL is not case sensitive, so the above line could be composed as:

Select * From Name_of_table

However your SQL explanations are simpler to peruse on the off chance that you write the essential words in uppercase letters. The decisive words in the lines above are SELECT and FROM. The indicator (*) signifies "All Records". The variable Name_of_table is the name of a table in your database. So the entire line peruses:

"SELECT all the records FROM the table called Name_of_table"

You don't need to choose all the records from your database. You can simply select the sections that you require. For instance, in the event that we needed to choose simply the first name and surname segments from this table, we can determine that in our SQL String:

"SELECT f_name, s_name FROM tb_customer_records";

At the point when this SQL proclamation is executed, just the f_name and s_name segments from the database will be returned. There are a considerable measure more SQL charges to get used to, and you'll meet a greater amount of them as you come. For the time being, we're simply selecting all the records from our table.

Inserting A Record

To add records to a table in your database, you utilize pretty much the same code as done a while ago. The main thing that needs to change is your SQL proclamation. The steps we're going to be take are:

1. Open an association with MySql
2. Specify the database we need to open
3. Set up a SQL Statement that can be utilized to add records to the database table
4. Use mysql_query( ) once more, yet this time to add records to the table
5. Close the association

The syntax of the query is as follows:

INSERT INTO name_of_table (Column/s) VALUES (value/s for sections)

Anyhow, attempt to run your code now, and check whether its all meeting expectations appropriately. You ought to observe that you now have two records in your database table.

Creating A Table

You can make tables utilizing SQL (and entire databases), and indicate the fields you need to make in the table. In any case, doing it along these lines is not proposed. We have a tendency to overlook which fields are in the table, their information sorts, which field is the essential keys, and which ones are assigned to NULL. On the off chance that you can get a grasp of visual devices like phpmyadmin, then this can be much simpler for you to comprehend and do.

To make a table, you can utilize the CREATE word (known as a statement, in database terminology). Here's the SQL to make the basic location book we've been utilizing. This accepts that the database itself as of now exists, and that the PHP code to open an association has as of now been composed:

$my_sql="create TABLE Customerrecords
(
ID int(7) NOT NULL auto_increment,

```
f_name varchar(50) NOT NULL,
s_name varchar(50) NOT NULL,
email_id varchar(50),
PRIMARY KEY (ID),
UNIQUE id (ID)
)";
mysql_query($my_sql);
```

Updating A Record

You can likewise overhaul a record in your table. Of course, the word UPDATE is utilized for this. Here's a sample:

$my_sql = "UPDATE Customerrecords SET email_id = "email_address" WHERE f_name = 'Jack' and s_name = 'Wright'";

After the expression UPDATE, you require the name of the table you need to update. At that point you require an alternate keyword: SET. After the word SET, you write the name of the column you need to change. In the SQL above, we're changing the email id. Anyway, recognize the WHERE provision. We've detailed that the record to change ought to have the f_name of Jack and the s_name of Wright.

Deleting A Record

On the off chance that you need to erase a record in a table, utilize the DELETE keyword. This can be performed in the following manner:

$my_sql = "DELETE FROM Customerrecords WHERE f_name = "Jack" AND s_name = 'Wright'";

After the DELETE word, you require FROM. At that point you write the name of the table. Next, you have to tag which record you need to erase. It's a decent thought to verify your WHERE statement is going to be a unique value.

www.ingramcontent.com/pod-product-compliance
Lightning Source LLC
LaVergne TN
LVHW022308060326
832902LV00020B/3345